Become a Successful Consultant

BECOME A SUCCESSFUL CONSULTANT

Raymond Hebson

foulsham

LONDON · NEW YORK · TORONTO · SYDNEY

foulsham

Yeovil Road, Slough, Berkshire SL1 4JH

ISBN 0-572-01500-3

Printed in Great Britain by St Edmundsbury Press Ltd,
Bury St Edmunds, Suffolk

CONTENTS

INTRODUCTION

Starting a business — any business — is a major step in a person's life. Advice about doing this is available from many sources, but much of it is based on the assumption that new enterprises will be concerned with goods rather than with services — if not actually manufacturing them, then processing or selling them. Yet the sale of your services as a consultant, working to solve other people's problems, can be very rewarding in both money and job satisfaction.

The two essentials

If you envisage becoming a self-employed consultant in your own specialised field, you will need to recognise at the outset that if the venture is to succeed it is necessary to

(a) provide marketable services and
(b) sell them profitably.

This may seem obvious; but the two requirements call for different abilities. Provision of consultancy services of marketable quality requires technical skill and knowledge of a high calibre, while selling those services — and, indeed, running the enterprise as a profitable concern — call for commercial and managerial expertise sufficient to meet and beat competition. These two abilities — one technical and the other commercial — do not necessarily co-exist in the same person. Most people will be able to think of someone of their acquaintance — maybe a garage mechanic — who, having acquired considerable skill at his job while working for someone else, has set up in business on his own account and then failed for lack of commercial knowledge. He was technically efficient as a mechanic, but he did not know how to cost his services, make business decisions, organise his stock or get in his money. He possessed only one of the abilities which his self-employed position demanded.

In some cases no problem will arise. If you are thinking of becoming a management consultant it is reasonable to assume that you will have the necessary management skills to run the consultancy, though you may not possess the right aptitude to cope with day-to-day administrative work, which may have to be done by someone else. Or, to take an entirely different case, you may be a budding consultant starting business with a thoroughly trustworthy partner to whom the running of the business can safely be left. But, however provided, commercial ability will have to be available if your business is to stand any reasonable chance of success. Those who — like our garage mechanic — are minded to get along on the strength of their technical skills alone, without any idea of how to run a business, are liable to be defeated by their competitors, and even by competitors less technically advanced than themselves.

Working from home

Most newcomers to the world of consultancy will start by working from home. In this connection 'from home' is more appropriate than 'at home' because, as we shall see in the section called 'The right working environment', a number of factors are relevant to the places at which consultancy work is done, and comparatively few consultants are able to do all their work without leaving their homes.

PART ONE
LIFE AS A CONSULTANT

WHAT IS A CONSULTANT?

It may be that the derivation of the word 'consultant' is of little interest except to linguists and pedants. But as linguists and pedants are very welcome to buy and read this book it seems reasonable to meet their requirements. The word comes from the Latin verb *consulere*, which, perhaps not surprisingly, means 'to consult'.

Of greater importance than the derivation is the definition to be used for the purposes of this book. Consultancy as a business can cover a virtually unlimited range of technical and commercial services, so the definition should not be too specific in that respect. The following is offered as suitable to our context. A consultant is an independent qualified person who:

(a) identifies problems;
(b) investigates them;
(c) recommends action; and
(d) helps to implement the recommendations.

The meaning of 'Independent'

'Independent' involves non-alignment with, for instance, suppliers of materials and equipment and indeed with anyone whose interests are, or could be, adverse to those of the consultant's client. Thus a consultant might make an agreement with a computer supplier entitling the consultant to commission on equipment sold to his clients; but if he did so he would no longer have the right to claim to be independent. But situations are not always clear-cut. Some organisations call their sales representatives 'consultants'. They are certainly not independent, as they are not permitted to recommend the products of their employers' rivals. Therefore they are not consultants within our definition.

Losing independence can happen in other ways also. Some of these will be considered later, but another obvious case is that in which the consultant becomes too friendly with his client's employees and feels obliged to take their part against him. This is not fair to the client; he is not paying the consultant to be someone else's mouthpiece. If employment problems are within the scope of your consultancy assignment, then you must present your recommendations to the client from a position of non-involvement.

Knowing why as well as how

The word 'qualified' in our definition also calls for explanation. It does not envisage any specific qualification in a given field; it would be absurd, for instance, to suggest that no one except a chartered or certified accountant could possibly be capable of solving accountancy problems. What the word means is that the consultant should be qualified to do the job for which he is being hired. Generally speaking his qualification will consist of a well-balanced mixture of theoretical and practical knowledge which is relevant to the problems to be solved. To this there will, of course, be exceptions; a pure theorist may well be able to think his way through the complexities which constitute the problem. On the other hand, it is unlikely that someone without any theoretical knowledge — someone who has learned his trade entirely by practical experience or in some other empiric way — will be able to cope with problems at consultancy level. This is because as a consultant you need to know *why* as well as *how* and to be able to explain the reasoning to your client.

Do you have what it takes?

At this stage, as an intending consultant, you should ask yourself some questions. First of all, can you be

1. professional?
2. competitive?
3. persistent?
4. disciplined?
5. reliable?

And then, can you

a. listen?
b. question rather than just accept?
c. dig out facts not supplied?
d. think out solutions clearly and logically?
e. explain them and your reasoning?
f. avoid personal prejudices?
g. talk to clients on level terms?
h. keep abreast of change?
j. see a tough assignment through?
k. remain solvent?

The first set of questions is designed to find out whether you have a general ability to run a business and the second set is intended to find out whether consultancy work is the right business for you. It is most unlikely that many people will be able to give an unqualified 'yes' or 'no' to every question. But many situations in life develop in shades of grey, rather than pure black or white, and the interrogation will have served its purpose if it has alerted your mind to the approaches and attitudes which you as a self-employed consultant will need to adopt. To sum up: consultancy is for those who think and analyse; it is not for those who accept and plod.

THE ICY BLAST — GOING IT ALONE

Life as a consultant is a life of problems — other people's. It can be interesting and exciting — or boring and predictable — it depends on your approach. And the right approach is essential if the business is to succeed.

Discarding the dependent mentality

To many people the main attraction of starting a consultancy is that of being self-employed. No longer will they have an employer, whether large and remote or small and local, to order them around. No; they will be able to do everything to suit themselves and feel completely free. They will be able to shop when they wish, and have their holidays when they wish, without being forced to follow the crowd. In reality this freedom may turn out to be illusory: clients can at times be just as demanding as the hardest of employers.

To get a consultancy — or, indeed, any kind of business — on its feet it is necessary to attune your mind to the new way of life. The dependent mentality of an employee must be discarded and replaced by a sense of independence and confidence. As a new consultant you must learn to deal with clients and prospective clients on level terms — even self-satisfied and imperious ones, whose characteristics are often a veneer concealing shortcomings in ability and personality.

Striking the right balance

The consultant must strike the right balance between servility and arrogance. This may be difficult to achieve, but it must be done.

The consequences of erring too far in either direction can be disastrous. A consultant who is obsequious — 'your humble servant' — is not only destroying any chance of selling his services profitably; he is also destroying the very platform from which, as a trusted adviser, he will need to operate. To be of real use in your chosen field you will have to be able to tell clients the truth — and sometimes the very unpalatable truth — about themselves and their operations and to advise them about changes. This simply cannot be done from a grovelling position — however sound your analysis and reasoning may be.

Erring in the opposite direction, if your approach is overconfident and arrogant then this is likely to make a poor impression. You need to remind yourself that the earth had been in existence for millions of years before you came on the scene and will doubtless continue for more millions after you have gone. To put things in perspective, the world will survive without your services: if they are to be sold they must be sold on their merits.

Losing the 'wage slave' mentality

Emerging from the security of paid employment can be like stepping out into an icy blast. Not only does an employer provide salary or wages, he provides many other benefits besides. Often these will include a comfortable private office and a company car. But even those who do not enjoy benefits like these will still have had the protection of their employer's 'umbrella' in other ways. For instance an employee does not usually have to look for work; it is provided for him. His salary is paid even when he is ill. His income tax is dealt with under the PAYE system. His earnings are not chargeable with VAT. He does not have to prepare his own accounts or provide his own workplace. Nor, in the majority of cases, does he have to bear an employer's responsibility for those who work under him.

In short, the employer often provides a total environment, in which the employee can feel relatively safe and secure. Stepping out into consultancy, as an ex-employee you will have to create your own environment in which to thrive.

Consultancy can present a very attractive career for independent-minded women. Indeed, many women are proving increasingly successful as consultants in areas once considered exclusively male preserves. Fitting in consultancy work with domestic responsibilities may present a problem, but problems are there to be solved, and good consultants of either sex are expert at doing just that.

PLANNING TO START A CONSULTANCY

Many people who go into business on their own account do so without any clear objectives. Do they have some vague idea of making a fortune? Or of leading a civilised life? Or (most likely) do they expect both? Unfortunately, these two goals often turn out to be mutually exclusive. Building up a business can be very hard work, especially if the sphere of activity is a highly competitive one. So every individual should think long and hard about what he is seeking, but in doing so he should reflect on the possibility of an ill-considered or half-hearted effort resulting in failure and serious financial loss.

Is there a big enough demand?

In setting out to be a consultant your first step should be to make an honest assessment of your knowledge and expertise and to try to decide whether it is likely to prove saleable and, if so, to whom and for how much. A fund of highly specialised knowledge is only an asset, viewed from a business standpoint, if people are prepared to pay for it. Might there be adverse factors outside your control? Might there, for instance, be a lack of demand because too many other people have the same knowledge? Or your expertise might be out of date, superseded by technical developments or even just by fashion. To take an obvious case, there can be little demand for consultants who can drive trams. This skill is simply not saleable in the UK.

Identifying your market

If, as an intending consultant, you are satisfied that what you can offer is relevant to today's world, and that there is likely to be a demand rather than an over-supply, your next step is to identify the market. Who will want your consultancy services? Former employers? Large groups? Small businesses? Firms in a particular area — or in a particular trade? An expert in distilling Scotch whisky is hardly likely to prosper in an area in which there are no stills. At this planning stage it is information that is needed, though hopefully you will be seeking business before long.

It makes good sense to list the potential clients to be approached and to try to find out (by ringing them up, if necessary) the name of the appropriate person at each. Letters can then be sent to them, setting out briefly and clearly what your new consultancy will offer and enquiring whether their company might be interested. An individually typed letter will create a better impression than a printed one. If you do not have access to a word-processor you can have the letters typed at a word-processing bureau. Sometimes it may not be necessary to write; perhaps you already have close contacts at some of the firms on the list and can telephone to find out whether they might be interested in your consultancy services. In any case, you should remember that the establishment of a new business presents a golden opportunity to get in touch with potential clients with a positive message to impart. When the business has been established for some time it is often difficult to find something with sufficient impact to justify re-establishing contact.

Aim for realistic goals

The result of all this writing and telephoning will be to provide some information as to whether or not you can expect a worthwhile volume of consultancy work in the early days. At best, the contacts will have resulted in some firm promises of work. At worst, there will have been no response at all. This does not necessarily mean that the consultancy will fail; it means that further effort is needed to research the market and present yourself in a more favourable light.

You should have goals and aim for them, but they should always be clear and realistic; it is no use professing skills which you do not possess or seeking business which you cannot handle. Being dishonest with both yourself and potential clients is a recipe for disaster.

THE RIGHT WORKING ENVIRONMENT

The scope of consultancy work is infinitely variable and there is no hard and fast rule about where the work should be done. As a consultant you will not usually be in a position to decide that you will have a fixed place of business from where you will normally operate during working hours. Various factors have a bearing on your workplace and the place at which you will carry out an assignment for a client is a matter of mutual arrangement. The client may wish the job to be done at his own premises but be unable to provide adequate working space for you. It therefore sometimes happens that the job has to be fitted in while one of the client's staff is ill or on holiday. In such a case you should co-operate in trying to work out a mutually satisfactory arrangement. It is certainly *not* a satisfactory arrangement if you are so cramped that you cannot work properly or if your presence causes dislocation so that the client's employees cannot get on with their work. Another problem is interruptions; for instance, if you are faced with a telephone which rings frequently for some absent person and can only be silenced by answering it yourself, then the position is unacceptable and should be discussed with the client.

Dealing with circumstances

Normally your requirement will be a clear desk at which you can work without interruption, but this is a very broad generalisation, and much depends on circumstances. For instance, your assignment, or more likely part of it, may be to restore a chaotic workplace to a tidy and functional state. Disarray can run away with money, especially if it is coupled with uncertainty about the nature and quantity of stock and equipment which the confusion conceals. Some managements do not possess the ability or patience to deal with this themselves so they entrust the task to a consultant. Therefore your first job will be to organise your own working space where you can put papers down and hopefully write on them. The next step will depend on the exact nature of the problem, and you will have to decide for yourself what you should do. However, working out one's own programme is an interesting facet of consultancy life. If the workplace is full of jumble, attention should be given to ascertaining what major items (i.e. bulky or valuable ones) are to be dealt with. They should be listed, preferably in some classified form which facilitates discussion with the client. The rest of the items should be given a general description. Do they consist mainly of scrap metal? Or papers? Or old furniture? You should aim at helping the client to decide what to do. For instance, if heavy or awkward items have to be moved as part of the operation, the client will have to provide the necessary labour.

Determining your status

One problem which frequently arises when a consultant works at his client's premises is misunderstanding about the consultant's status and what he is supposed to be doing. Many employees have never come across consultants and are unfamiliar with their function. Strictly speaking they should be briefed by the client rather than by the consultant, but sometimes this is not done until the consultant presses the point, and perhaps not adequately even then if the client is not very articulate. So you may have to introduce yourself.

Relevant employees — the ones with whom you will come in contact — should at least be told that you are not a new employee but a consultant who has been engaged to do a specific job for the firm and will appreciate their co-operation. How far they will be told the exact nature of the job will depend largely on the client's wishes and should be discussed with him. Usually staff are very helpful to a consultant when they know who he is and why he is there; indeed, they are on their mettle.

A place of your own

It has to be accepted that it is not always possible to work on the client's premises. Lack of space, as we have seen, may prevent this; or the assignment may, for security reasons, be better done elsewhere. Or there may be a need for laboratory or workshop facilities which the client does not possess. In such a case you may be able to work at home or at your own office, laboratory or workshop. Establishing your own workplace is described under 'Setting up your own premises' in Part Two.

MARKETING FOR THE LEADING EDGE

As we saw in the Introduction, ample advice is available for those who have goods to sell. On the subject of marketing, book upon book has been written, and lecture after lecture delivered, but in almost every case the emphasis has been on goods rather than on services. Indeed, to such an extent have services been neglected that the intending consultant might be forgiven for wondering whether his services will need to be marketed at all.

Anticipating client demand

Yet effective marketing is vital whatever type of consultancy work is envisaged. In the section 'Planning to start a consultancy' consideration was given to an approach to likely clients at the planning stage in the hope of learning something about the potential demand. The contacts which were made at that stage will, of course, be followed up when you have actually commenced business, but even if they bring in a satisfactory volume of work you must not be content to rest on your laurels. Marketing is a forward-looking activity, and you must strive continuously to find out what, within your ability (or potential ability) to deliver, is likely to be required, and how the requirements can profitably be met.

There are numerous aspects to this. Are there, for instance, geographical limits within which clients are likely to be found or beyond which you will not be able to operate profitably? And what is the strength of the competition? Even if there are no other consultants providing similar services in your area, are the relevant requirements being met in other ways, such as through trade organisations or chambers of commerce? Every single factor which could have a bearing on marketability must be taken into account and its possible effect must be periodically reviewed.

Staying competitive

What are the relative strengths of yourself and your rivals? How can your own strengths and other people's weaknesses be exploited to the best advantage? Sometimes the weaknesses do not apply to the standard of the services provided; they may relate, for instance, to incompatible personalities or to delay on the part of a consultant in coming to grips with problems. It is a good thing to belong to organisations in the areas or in the professions or trades from which you aim at deriving business. The secretary of such an organisation may be a useful person to know if his members are likely to need consultancy help. If there are any relevant trade periodicals they will help you to keep up to date with what is happening in your chosen field. If you do *not* keep up to date you are developing a weakness for your rivals to exploit.

If your work is centred on a particular trade or industry it must not be expected that a job well done will automatically lead to recommendations. This is because a firm which has found you an excellent consultant in a particular field is hardly likely to broadcast your name to its competitors.

As time goes on it should be increasingly possible to identify the areas in which your own services have a competitive edge. When this has been done, every opportunity to inform clients and prospective clients should be seized. But competitive edges can be blunted, and you can be sure that rival consultants will not hesitate to take advantage.

Target your advertising

It is especially important that advertising should be aimed at the right places. A press advertisement is a waste of time and money unless it reaches potential clients. A direct mail shot might be better, depending on how it is worded and how the recipients are chosen. However, it is quite possible to send out 10,000 glossy brochures and get no response. It is also possible to send a dozen letters to carefully chosen firms and to be rewarded with an encouraging amount of new business. But letters, if they are to have a good chance of success, must be well worded and neatly typed on well-designed headed paper. An approach anything less than this is liable to do more harm than good. If the names of suitable recipients are not known, a local reference library may have the right directories. If not, it may be necessary to visit a city where there is a commercial library.

Whatever form the advertising takes it should be undertaken in a discreet and professional way. Some professions and associations place restrictions on advertising by their members, and a consultant who belongs to one of these should either abide by its rules or resign his membership. Trouble with your own professional body for over-stepping the mark may not be fatal to building up a consultancy practice, but it does not pay in the long term to make enemies from the start.

The first contact

When the stage is reached for discussing your services with prospective clients, you will need to present a business card giving your name, address and telephone number and a brief description of the services offered. You may also find it useful to be supplied with well-produced printed matter giving further details, but you will probably discover that, if you produce it during a discussion, the exchange of views will get bogged down while the prospect makes a half-hearted attempt to study the literature. Therefore, it is generally better to leave your brochure with him when departing or send it on later with a covering letter.

It is vital to make a good impression on first contact. Take care with your appearance and be as professional and helpful as possible. Avoid idle chat — it will create the wrong impression.

ESTABLISHING A GOOD CLIENT RELATIONSHIP

Clients, fortunately, are not perfect beings. If they were they would not need consultants! And one of their imperfections is that they do not always tell the consultant what the real problem is. In business, as in life generally, many people have a strong tendency to go on doing things as they have always done them, perhaps rather mindlessly and with no positive wish to change. Yet the consultant whom they have called in is an agent of change; he has to be if he is to bring about improvement.

Getting started

Against such a negative background, which fortunately does not apply in every case, you will have to try to winkle out what the real trouble is. Perhaps the client does not know or is too afraid or too ashamed to tell the real truth. This should not be held against him; as his consultant it is your job to put matters right, not to dwell on the shortcomings of your client.

The scope of a consultant's services is, within the bounds of his knowledge, completely flexible. Therefore it is unnecessary for you to offer the client anything so formal — and perhaps frightening — as 'a survey', 'an appraisal' or 'a report' if you believe that the best way to get the job started is to have an informal discussion round the table or on-site to enable you to get the information you require and form some idea about what needs to be done. You can then, if you think it necessary, reassure the client, who may be worried about entering into an open-ended commitment for consultancy fees. For instance, you can give a firm quotation (based, perhaps, on one day's fees, or one week's, depending on circumstances) for clarifying the position as far as possible within the time on which the quotation is based. Having undertaken this basic assessment you should then have a better grasp of what is involved and should be ready to take part in an informed discussion about solving the client's problems. You should also be able to indicate what your own contribution to the operation might be and what it would be likely to cost. The client should be made fully aware of the availability of *all* your consultancy services — identifying, investigating, recommending, helping to implement — but discretion should be used as to how much of this he is expected to order at any given time.

The client is always right!

Not every enquiry matures into an assignment. Sometimes the 'prospect' will not even be there when you call by appointment. He will have left no message about where he is or when he will be back. Or he may see you but put you off, or perhaps he will try to drive a hard bargain on the ground that he cannot finalise any arrangements without the concurrence of a hard person, kept unseen, in the background. A further possibility is that he will want to spend hours in reiteration and recapitulation, always coming back to the same conclusion (reached, of course, without the handicap of logical analysis) that no one can really do anything to help and events will have to be left to take their course.

Analysis is the key to this situation. While it is the privilege of the client — who, after all, pays the piper — to reach conclusions on grounds which could be shown by sound reasoning to be utterly misconceived, as the consultant you must *not* reach conclusions in this way. It is you who must bring an analytical mind to bear on the problem, and you must not lose patience if your muddled client cannot match your own standard of reasoning. Raised voices will solve nothing — and they will certainly not enhance your reputation as a calm solver of problems.

The contract letter

Let us assume that all has gone well. The preliminary discussions are over, and the client wants to use your services as a consultant. What happens next? It is not good business, nor is it good for morale, to be constantly arguing with the client. It is a better idea, when you are being given your instructions (or 'remit' in the language of consultancy) to discuss any points which might conceivably arise and get them settled. But is it enough just to make an oral arrangement? Or ought there to be a formal contract?

Between two business people who know and trust each other, and have worked together for a long time, oral arrangements ('my word is my bond') are probably sufficient. But in the early days, before acquaintances have matured, such arrangements can lead to misunderstandings. On the other hand, if a forbidding looking and over-complicated contract form were placed before the worried client for signature, he might well be frightened off. So the best course, once the arrangements have been agreed with the client, is to embody them in a letter. Then at that time, if it is thought necessary, a solicitor can be asked to look over it.

The contract letter should always cover the following points:

1. *Names and addresses of both parties.* If the letter is written on your printed letter paper, and starts with the client's name and address, this requirement will be met.
2. *The job which the consultant is required to do.* A clear statement, with enough detail for both parties to be sure about what you are undertaking to do.
3. *The fee (if a fixed sum) or the rate at which it will be calculated.* This rate may be hourly, daily, weekly or monthly. Whatever the basis of calculation it will probably be found convenient to invoice the fee monthly unless the client prefers some other arrangement. Again, this should be made clear in the letter; it is unwise to assume that the client will know when to expect fee invoices. And what about VAT? No room should be left for doubt about whether the quoted fee includes or excludes VAT. It should be stated in the letter.
4. *Where the consultant is to work.* This subject has been dealt with under 'The right working environment'. In discussing the arrangements with the client it should be borne in mind that in the early stages of an assignment it is often better to work at the client's premises so as to have access to any facts and figures which may be needed. Later, when this facility is no longer required, it may be possible to save travel and other expenses by working at your own home or office. But there should be a clear understanding with the client which should be stated in the letter.
5. *The facilities (if any) to be provided at the client's premises.* A desk, as discussed earlier, should be a clear one, as otherwise you will be fighting a losing battle (and have to take your mind off the assignment) to avoid getting the client's papers mixed with yours. If other facilities will be needed, such

as access to a laboratory or workshop, assistance of staff, or use of a computer, these requirements should be clearly and accurately set out in the letter.

6. *Arrangements about expenses.* Who is to pay these? Frequently it is the client, and although consultants' expenses seldom seem to be a bone of contention, it is sensible to have expenses arrangements clearly agreed and confirmed in the letter. Hotels, restaurants, trains and taxis present no problems because you will claim the actual amount paid. Car expenses are a more likely source of trouble, and a mileage rate should be agreed at the outset. This should be a rate which takes account of all expenses in connection with the car (including garaging and depreciation) and not merely petrol and oil. The client may already have a satisfactory rate applicable to car users in his own organisation and you may decide to use this. The client can hardly complain that the rate is excessive if this method is adopted! But you should keep a note of the agreed rate with your time records; you will need it when you come to make out your fee invoice. If you have several assignments current at the same time, and you rely on memory for mileage rates, or if you recorded these on scraps of paper which have in the meantime been lost, you may have to go back to the client to confirm the rate, in which case your efficient image will probably suffer.

Anticipating any pitfalls

There may be other points that will need to be included in the letter. But even though it must be precise in wording it should not be unfriendly in tone. After all, it is an amicable business deal which is being set up, not (one hopes) a hostile law case. However, a word of caution is necessary here: if in the letter you introduce some new terms or conditions which were not agreed in discussion, the client may reject them and both parties may finish up without any contract at all.

Sometimes consultant and client agree on a fixed period, such as three months, for the carrying out of an assignment. Unfortunately, this arrangement can misfire, because problems which were not envisaged at the outset may crop up, and the client, having made a contract favourable to himself, may not be disposed to renegotiate it. He may well argue that the consultant, with his experience, should have foreseen the possibility of new problems and covered this aspect in the original contract letter. A consultant must always honour his contract, so before entering into an arrangement of this kind you should try to identify the likely areas of trouble and seek to exclude them from the scope of your fixed-term fee.

Guarding your integrity

In general, clients employ consultants to provide specialised skill and knowledge not otherwise available to them. But sometimes a consultant may be called in to cover the absence of a member of staff or to give an independent opinion on a particular point. Here lie the seeds of possible trouble. Some managements do not take kindly to opinions which do not accord with their own, and they may indicate beforehand what they expect the consultant to say. Any attempt to commit you in this way, before you have even had an opportunity to study the problem, must be resisted, even if the assignment is lost as a result. If you are to stay in business as a consultant, then you must safeguard your independence and reputation.

This is not the only pitfall awaiting a consultant with a weak will. Even worse is allowing yourself to be exposed to blackmail. It is not unknown for a consultant to be persuaded to overlook a particular fact, or to leave something out or put something in when making his report, so that someone in the client's organisation may gain an advantage (or, more likely, escape a disadvantage). Perhaps a weak-willed consultant might be tempted to yield to pressure of this kind, falsely confident in the belief that the person exerting it could not implicate the consultant without involving himself also. But quite apart from the ethical considerations in a case of this kind, which are overwhelming, to succumb to such pressures can be a bad commercial risk. This is because the instigator may already be in trouble himself, and be seeking a means of diverting attention elsewhere, by revealing the consultant's part in the deception.

DEVELOPING CLIENT RELATIONSHIPS

Good luck is welcome at any time, especially when you are starting your own business. But when the consultancy is actually in being, and assignments are being undertaken, more than luck will be needed. The development of good relationships with the clients will be essential to future success. It is perhaps unnecessary to say that you the consultant's aim should be to satisfy your clients, and that one thing which they will all expect is improvement. Otherwise they would not be using your services. Clients will not be interested in, and should not be burdened with, your personal troubles.

There are three positive ways in which you can establish and maintain the reputation of your consultancy with your clients. The first is by ensuring the technical quality of your work; the second is by being thoroughly reliable; and the third is by achieving good presentation. Let us look at these in more detail.

Demonstrable technical quality

If you set out to be a consultant in a particular field, you will be expected to have expert knowledge, saleable against competition. Moreover, you must talk sensibly to your clients, answer their questions and make recommendations. If it emerges that you know less about your subject than your client you are unlikely to derive further business from that source. Indeed, if your knowledge is only equal to that of your client you can expect the same result unless the client is himself seeking a second opinion. Again, knowledge is of little value without the ability to apply it. A theoretical work-out of a client's problem may be very erudite, but the client will not want to pay for it unless it also helps him to know how to act.

Total reliability

A promise to be at your client's office at 9.30 on Monday morning should be kept — unless you are prevented by some emergency such as illness or accident. Even then the client should be contacted as soon as possible, by someone else if you are unable to do so. The client, already inconvenienced by your non-arrival, should not be left to do the chasing. An employee who is ill can send in a sick note and be assured that others will cover for him. But as a self-employed consultant you must make your own arrangements to ensure that clients are kept informed.

Unreliability can creep in in other ways also. Failure to return telephone calls is an obvious example. Another is failure without explanation to submit a report (or to complete whatever else you are supposed to be doing) by the promised date. Some employees become surprisingly slack when they work for easy-going employers. However, it must never be assumed that clients are easy-going: some may be, but self-discipline should not be relaxed on that account. A consultant expects to be paid, even if the client is easy-going. And that client, despite his laxity, is entitled to get what he pays for.

Superb presentation

While it is quite possible to be efficient and yet send out badly-typed letters, or arrive for work unsuitably dressed, such manifestations of indifference do not *look* efficient and tend to create an adverse impression. If the consultancy work is to be done in a client's office, you should dress soberly and professionally unless and until you establish that a less formal style is acceptable. If you need to work down a mine you will dress to go down a mine.

If it is necessary for clients to call on you, then your location should be clearly indicated on your card or on other literature — a map showing the nearest car parks would be useful. And you will need to be found quickly and easily in the alphabetical phone books and the yellow pages. You should study your entries and consider whether extra ones are necessary. British Telecom have used Humpty Dumpty to exemplify a common problem — should you look under H or D? Preferably (if Humpty Dumpty wants people to find him) under either.

Whenever the client has to be informed about the progress of the work this should be presented professionally and done in a considerate way. The client does not want to be informed every time some figures are added up on the calculator. But he does want to know, and promptly, when significant progress is being made towards solving a problem. How to do this without becoming a nuisance is a question of judgement. It will depend on the client's accessibility and the pressures on his time, which brings us to another point — when should reports be oral, and when in writing? This cannot be easily answered. If the client is available for discussions every day, or at all events frequently, then it will not be necessary to put as much on paper as if he were absent. But when a mass of detail has to be presented it should be put on paper. Without going too deeply into the field of information layout and retrieval, which is a subject for a separate book in itself, you can ensure that the information is so arranged that it can be easily understood. The client should not be faced with so much information, in dauntingly irretrievable form, that he might as well not have any.

Another occasion for a written report is when the client has to be told something which you as consultant might be blamed for failing to report. It is very easy for a busy client to forget, or for an unscrupulous one to 'forget', that he has been told anything. You should report your findings and conclusions as simply and as clearly as possible — there is no need to be over-formal or over-fussy.

Building client confidence

Decisions will be necessary about these and other matters as business develops. Large clients, for instance, will be welcome if they provide a worthwhile volume of business. But as in many other fields of activity it is unwise to have all your eggs in one basket. The danger is that a large client may virtually become an employer and destroy independence. If a relationship with a client shows signs of developing in this way a suitable opportunity should be taken to put matters right. One way of doing this, unless you have promised full-time availability, would be for you to excuse yourself for an occasional day or afternoon — for which, of course the large client would not be charged — for the express purpose of attending to the pressing problems of other clients.

When you have finished your assignment, even if you have done it well, you should not look for praise, or even thanks, on your departure. Nowadays business is conducted more impersonally than it used to be, and a client who pays the bill reckons that he has done enough. However, you should certainly not infer from the lack of laudation that the client is dissatisfied. In any case, if the client's working papers remain in your hands after the assignment has been completed, you will have an opportunity to enquire whether all is well when you return the papers.

In some quarters it is considered smart to impress a client at all costs, even if this involves misleading him. It certainly is not smart, and it may destroy such confidence as the client has in your ability as a consultant. Even without self-inflicted troubles of this kind you can never be really sure that the right message is getting through to your clients and that you are acquiring the reputation of your choosing. So no apology is offered for repeating the oft-quoted words of Robert Burns: 'O wad some Pow'r the giftie gie us to see oursels as others see us'.

Outstaying your welcome

Sometimes your consultancy assignment will come to an abrupt end, usually after the client has received an invoice for fees. Yesterday, before the invoice arrived, all was well and there was no sign of impending trouble. But today the client has discovered that he can do without your assistance. He may be very polite and say that he will be in touch with you when he wants help again — which may, of course, be never!

You have outstayed your welcome. Sometimes this is due to no fault of your own; the client, unmindful of the accruing liability for fees, may have encouraged you to stay. But in other cases you may realise with hindsight that if you had been a little more perceptive you might have handled the situation better. The seeds of trouble are liable to be sown if

(a) you have been working on the assignment for some time without indicating that you are getting any nearer a solution to the problems; or
(b) the problems have been solved, you have stayed on to help to implement the recommendations, but have not given any indication as to how long this is likely to take.

In each of these cases there is an obvious failure of communication, though this is only part of the story. Case (a) suggests that you might have become bogged down, because if you had achieved a breakthrough for the client then presumably you would have said so. It is not fair to the client to get bogged down but still continue to run up fees. It would be more sensible to take a break from the assignment and come back to it with a clearer mind. In case (b) you might, depending on need, have been wiser to come in less frequently. Someone who is paying does not like an open-ended situation and welcomes a sign of this kind that the drain is starting to diminish.

However, when the end has come it serves no good purpose to reproach yourself. It is far better to think positively, not only to avoid the same thing happening with other clients but to try to regain the confidence of the client who has dispensed with your services. New Year is an excellent time to make peace — why not write to the client expressing the hope that all is well with him and wishing him a happy and successful year?

COPING WITH EMPLOYEES AND CUSTOMERS

The relationship between consultant and client has been considered: you should be neither arrogant nor subservient. But you will meet other people in the course of carrying out your assignments. Almost certainly you will meet some of the client's employees, and perhaps you will come into contact with customers as well. What should your strategy be?

Liaising with employees

It is hardly necessary to say that your consultancy assignment will be easier if you are on good terms with everyone. But it is unwise to go too far. You should adopt a friendly and helpful attitude to the client's employees so far as you can reasonably do so without getting yourself involved in something for which you have not been hired. There may come a time when you have to tell someone firmly that you are a consultant with a specific job to do, and you will find this easier if your have kept your distance. And there may also come a time when you have to report an employee to your client; if you have become over-friendly with that employee you will be faced with divided loyalties. This should not happen; your clear duty is to your client. And you must never get caught up in 'office politics'.

It can easily happen that, in the course of your assignment, you find an employee doing part of his job in an unduly labour-intensive way. If so, it may be sensible for you to ask the employee why he does the work that way. You may be rewarded with a reasoned explanation or (perhaps dependent to some extent on the manner of your approach) you may be faced with an indignant 'This is how

I've always done it' or 'This is the *right* way to do it!' Depending on the employee's reply you may or may not think fit to suggest a better way. With luck you may even get the employee to agree. But at least you have done the employee the courtesy of seeking his views before reporting the matter. You have not gone straight over the employee's head.

You must keep your mind clear on an important aspect of consultancy work: your primary duty is to solve problems, not to fix blame or get someone punished. Sometimes the two unhappily converge, as in a case in which a consultant, in trying to find out what is wrong, uncovers fraud. It can come as a profound shock, even to an experienced and realistic consultant, to discover that a trusted employee has been feathering his nest. If you are unfortunate enough to be confronted with such a situation, you must report to the client and leave him to decide what to do. A memorandum reporting suspected fraud might read like this:

> There has been a marked increase in the amount paid out for running the canteen, although the number of meals served has not risen and, as far as I can judge, neither has the amount of food in stock. The canteen management have not given me any satisfactory explanation or, indeed, any explanation at all apart from vague references to inflation. In my view this is an area in which tighter controls should be applied. The possibility might also be explored of entrusting the canteen management to an outside firm.

Customer strategy

So much for the client's employees; what about his customers? Perhaps you will not meet them, but sometimes it is necessary to talk to them in order to get information necessary to complete the consultancy assignment. If the client has not already done so you must make it clear to the customer that you are a consultant and not a member or employee of the firm. Some of the people you meet may be able — even keen — to supply goods or services which will prove useful in future assignments for other clients. But for the moment you must concentrate on working for the client who is paying and defer any potential benefits to a later date.

Some consultancy assignments continue for many years. Perhaps this is inevitable in exceptional cases, but there is no doubt that the impact of being an outsider diminishes as time goes on. You tend to become part of the scenery; you get drawn more and more into routine work which could perhaps be done by someone less highly paid. But you must be on your guard against getting too entrenched. The routine work may well be easier than the assignment which you are being paid to do, but you must not be tempted. For how can you justify a consultant's fees if you are doing an understrapper's job?

A CONSULTANT IS NOT AN EXECUTIVE

If you are a consultant who has previously been an executive you will have been accustomed to deciding what needs to be done and then getting on with it — or perhaps telling others to get on with it — without reference to anyone else. As a consultant you will need to adjust to your new role. If you are given a problem to solve you will need to go back to the client with the solution and get his approval — perhaps in writing if this is thought to be necessary — before putting the solution into effect. In some cases, of course, you may have the client's express permission — or even instructions — to 'do whatever is necessary' or words to that effect, but even so you will be wise if you tell the client what is happening. In giving you *carte blanche* — or appearing to do so — the client may not have envisaged the kind of steps which you may wish to take. To the client they may seem unorthodox; he may not like them, in which case it is sensible for him to have an opportunity of saying so and having the reasons for them explained.

Acting in the client's interests

There are, of course, occasions on which it is impossible to refer back to the client. A snap decision may be required to meet a deadline and instant communication with the client may not be feasible. Or the client may have been taken into intensive care in the middle of a project, leaving the consultant as the only person with sufficient knowledge of the project to carry it on. In such a situation you have an overriding duty to judge what is best in the client's interest (not your own) and act accordingly. If it is possible to have meaningful discussions with the client's other advisers (e.g.

accountants, solicitors, surveyors) and they are in a position to give useful advice, they should be consulted. If it is possible without detriment to keep open the client's options, or some of them, until he can be consulted, then this should be done. And you must remember that, although you may be in the driving seat during the emergency, you must revert to your original position as consultant as soon as the client is in command again. Some of the actions which you will have taken or authorised in the meantime may not be readily understood and approved and it is your duty as the consultant to explain and justify them.

One of the fascinations of consultancy work is encountering the unexpected. But exceptional situations, such as those which have just been described, must not blind you to the fact that the problems which as a consultant you have been hired to solve are those of the client, not your own, and you must be prepared to play second fiddle as long as the client is there to make the decisions. Sometimes your advice will be rejected. This should not be an occasion for flying into a rage; on the contrary, it should be used as an opportunity to show your maturity and resilience. You are not there to dictate, and there may be various reasons why your advice is unacceptable. These may be personal to the client himself, such as lack of courage to take the steps which have been recommended. Perhaps he is frightened of offending someone who matters. Or there may be valid reasons which are outside your technical scope.

Finding an acceptable solution

A good example of the last of these arose some years ago in the steel industry. A company manufactured bars for reinforcing concrete and from time to time experimented with new designs. One of these gave the company cause for concern, as they felt that there might be a risk of infringing someone else's patent. The company turned for advice to a consultant who was well versed in the law of patents and who expressed the view that the new design would, as the company had feared, infringe the patent. However, he felt it his duty to illustrate the point at issue by designing a different bar which he was confident the company could safely manufacture without infringing the patent. It was not put into production. Perfect though it might have been in its compliance with legal requirements, it would have been useless for reinforcing concrete.

That particular consultant's relationship with his client was not an ongoing one, so the rejection of his design marked the end of the matter. But if as a consultant you have a continuing relationship with a client then you are in a different position. If you are accustomed to giving advice to a client who suddenly starts to reject it, you can hardly be blamed for trying to ascertain the reason — not out of any wish to pry into the client's affairs, but to enable you, if there has been a change of policy, to work out more acceptable solutions in future.

Fitting in with management style

When you are on your client's premises, or in contact with your client's employees, it is very unwise for you to flaunt the fact that you are not yourself an employee. For instance, if you are working on premises, or in circumstances in which employees are forbidden to smoke, you will be very ill-advised to ignore this injunction, even though as a non-employee you are breaking no rule.

This advice applies even more strongly if you are retained, albeit on a consultancy basis, to stand in for an absent member of the staff or board, or you are carrying out professional work in circumstances in which you are almost an extra member of staff. In such circumstances you must still be guided by the general principles of consultancy conduct; you owe a duty to your client, and you must not incense your client's employees or get involved in their office politics. If you are placed in a position of authority you must exercise that authority and report any rejection of it. You should try to fit in with the management style of the client concern, be on good (but not too close) terms with your quasi-equals, seek their help when necessary and offer yours. To undertake a staff-type job on a consultancy basis can be an interesting and informative change from normal consultancy work; and where there are no rules for guidance there is no substitute for common sense.

PROBLEM SOLVING

As we have seen, solving other people's problems is what consultancy is about, so a book of this kind would be incomplete without some general guidance on the subject. It is a topic on which much has been said and written, and if you require more than this brief outline, you will find that there are specialised publications dealing with every aspect of the subject.

The following seven steps are suggested as a procedure for dealing with clients' problems:

1. Identify the problem

As we saw in the section 'Establishing a good client relationship', the client is not always capable of telling the consultant what the real problem is. So you will need to be able to 'look through' the client's own description, where necessary, to the reality which lies beneath.

2. Ascertain the amount at stake

This is an important part of the operation and it should not be deferred. A consultant who spends weeks or months working on the more interesting aspects of an assignment may in the long run have to admit to his client that there is little or nothing at stake. The client's reaction is likely to be 'You should have told me that in the first place. Why should I pay your fees?'

Whether or not he is right depends on all the circumstances. It must be inferred from his very action in engaging a consultant that he considered the matter important enough to justify the fees. But, having said that, his knowledge of the subject may have been so limited and his records in such disarray that he had no means of judging the scale of the problem. Yet he expected the consultant to do so.

This type of situation — working in the dark — is not uncommon in the early stages of a consultancy assignment. Therefore as a sensible consultant you must make the best possible estimate of the amount at stake as soon as you can. The estimate, and the difficulty in achieving accuracy, should be made known to the client, who will have to decide whether further consultancy fees can be risked in the hope that results will justify them. And if the client decides to take the plunge, you should keep him informed as the position becomes clearer and the worth of the fees can be better judged.

3. Establish the facts

Before the problem can be properly solved you need to be sure of the facts — as sure, that is, as is possible in the circumstances. No doubt the client will provide the facts as known to him and you will work on them on the assumption that they are correct unless, in the course of your work, you find them to be wrong. If they are substantially incorrect you should report that fact to the client and continue your work on the basis of the facts known by you to be correct.

But there will be times when some of the relevant facts are not available, and if you are to make progress at all, having tried and failed to get what is missing, you will have to work on assumptions. When this happens the client is entitled to know, and not merely to know that assumptions have had to be made; he should be told precisely what has been assumed and what missing information has given rise to the need for assumptions.

If the matter is anything of significance he should be told in writing. Many people seem to be reluctant to put anything in writing, perhaps due to laziness or to the inability to think and write logically. But the client ought to be given a chance to accept or reject your assumptions and especially to know the basis upon which the consultancy assignment will be proceeding. If as the consultant you fail to write, and the assumptions turn out to be totally wrong, you may be in serious trouble for having given utterly worthless advice. Here is an example of a precautionary memorandum to a client:

> I have not been able to find out anything about the cost of materials for the first batch because the records seem to have

been lost. I have therefore assumed the unit cost for the first batch to be the same as for the second. That is not very satisfactory, but it is the best that can be done in the circumstances. If the missing records can be found — or if together we can reconstitute them — I shall be pleased to recalculate the figures for the first batch.

4. Eliminate the irrelevant

Reference has been made to 'relevant' facts. As a consultant you may well find yourself overwhelmed with information, some of it relevant and some not. You must therefore sift the facts and decide which are relevant. If you take irrelevant matter into consideration you are unlikely to reach a valid conclusion.

5. Work out solutions

The inability of many clients to think their problems through properly, and the need for consultants to analyse, has already been mentioned. But what does this mean, and how do you go about it? A good definition of analysis is 'a separation into simple elements' and this is a very suitable description of the consultant's main function. But analysis will have different applications for different kinds of consultants, so let us take a simple example to show what we mean.

A consultant has formed the view that his client could get some useful business from Aberdeen if only he would bestir himself and go there. In that area there are several firms which would probably be very interested in what he has to offer. So the consultant advises his client to spend three days in Aberdeen and gives a list of the firms to the client's secretary, who arranges appointments for him. But the client, like many other people, erroneously thinks of Aberdeen as the back of beyond and is apprehensive about venturing into a foreign land where he may encounter language difficulties. The client will go by car so that he can carry some bulky exhibits in the boot. He asks the consultant how long it will take him to get there and how much cash he will need to carry. The consultant replies (based on his own last visit to Aberdeen some 20 years earlier) 'Oh, about ten hours, and take about £50'.

The consultant has not done his job. He has not thought, he has not analysed, and he has not given the sort of help for which the client is paying him. After all, it is at his recommendation that the client is going to Aberdeen, and he should be helping with the arrangements instead of giving an off-the-cuff, dismissive, don't-know-and-don't-care answer. A sensible course would have been to consult an up-to-date road atlas and work out the best route. If the client belonged to a motoring organisation and its assistance was needed it should have been obtained. The consultant should have calculated the number of miles of motorways and dual and single carriageways and applied suitable average speeds. He would have then been able precisely to say to his client: 'If you use the route which I suggest you can expect to spend about seven hours on the road, barring unforeseeable delays'.

On the subject of cash, the consultant's thought processes should have been along the following lines: Where will the client be staying? Will he be taking his wife? What does the hotel charge? Will it accept credit cards? If so, will it accept the particular ones which he has? Will he be entertaining any of the prospects? If so, how many? (If he is entertaining prospects, he must do it properly. Snack bars will not do!) Does the client eat a big lunch? What spending money will he need? Can he pay for petrol by credit card? If not, how much money will he need for fuel if he starts with a full tank? Has an allowance been made for contingencies? Or will he be skint if he breaks down on the way home?

The consultant should have got it right and reported on the lines of: 'Assuming that you will not be entertaining more than two people to dinner, that your hotel and petrol will be settled by credit cards, and that . . . (whatever other assumptions have been made) . . . you should find £250 enough, but if you run into problems your bank's agents are . . .'

Now helping the client to get to Aberdeen is not a matter of great moment, and no doubt he and his secretary would have sorted it out if the consultant had not. But it was the consultant who was asked, and having accepted the task it was his duty to discharge it in a professional and analytical way. This imaginary trip to Aberdeen has been given because it exemplifies the sort of approach which is needed and can be readily understood whatever your line of consultancy may be. The casual, the off-the-cuff, the homespun, must be rejected, and problems must be broken into their simple elements, just as the definition says.

The next example is not imaginary. A run-down company was acquired by a large group. Soon afterwards a member of the group management, visiting the company's works, was appalled to find it closed on a working day. When asked to explain, the managing director, who had been taken over with the business, said that it was a normal closure for routine maintenance. Asked why this could not be done at the weekend, he replied that it would cost too much. When he was asked what the extra cost would be, he said that he had no idea and added quite forcefully that it did not matter anyway, because as managing director it was his job to see that the company did not incur *any* unnecessary expense. So the head office man went away and made his own enquiries. He found, as he had expected, that the additional cost of having the work done at the weekend would have been minimal when set against the loss of production occasioned by the weekday closure. Faced with this, the managing director admitted that the idea of making such a comparison had not entered his head. Soon he was on his way out and the company was on its way up. The MD hadn't thought; he hadn't analysed. Consultants must think and consultants must analyse. Or they won't last long either.

6. Present the solution

The next stage is for you to present the solution or solutions (with guidance in choosing, if more than one) to those responsible for making the decision, who are usually the clients. Alternatives should be compared in money terms wherever possible.

On no account should you advocate a course which is morally indefensible. Man-made rules can, however, cause problems. It is undeniable that in some circumstances the infringement of such a rule is seen as the lesser of two evils. A simple example of this is risking a fine for unlicensed action when there is insufficient time to obtain a licence; and indeed in some circles a fine is regarded as the equivalent of a licence, differing from it only in procedure. There is also a further problem; many businesses have worldwide interests, and what is lawful in one country may be heavily penalised, perhaps for political reasons, in another. What should you the consultant do? It is certainly no part of your business to advise your clients to break the law, and if you know that a contemplated course of action is, or may be, illegal, you ought to warn your client about this, preferably in writing. If you are not sure, and feel that the projected course may infringe the law somewhere, but not necessarily in your own country, a sensible move is to make your misgivings known to the client with a suggestion that suitable advice be obtained from a lawyer of the country concerned.

7. Get a decision

If you have presented your recommendations adequately, with sound reasoning underlying them, there should be no need to try to save the decision-maker (the client) from himself. You may be superior to the client in your own technical field, but you are not entitled to assume that your judgement is sounder. So the responsibility of decision should be left where it lies without any attempt to arrogate it; the decision may be influenced by factors outside your scope, as we have already seen.

How to avoid time-wasting

We have now reached the stage at which your job is finished so far as the solution of the problem is concerned, though the client may need your assistance in implementing the recommendations. But before we leave the subject of problem-solving it is opportune to recall that, if you are to retain your clients, you must be competitive, which means that you must not waste time. The following suggestions will help in this respect.

(a) *Do not follow obvious non-starters through to logical conclusions.* The consultancy operation is not meant to provide the consultant with strenuous mental exercise; it is intended to help the client. There is, however, an important exception to this; it is sometimes necessary to pursue false reasoning to a conclusion if it is the only way to convince the client that it is false. But if too many non-starters are pursued to the bitter end the client is liable to become very uneasy and to remind you that you are not being paid to chase rainbows.

(b) *Akin to pursuing non-starters is failure to use tolerances.* If they apply, then use them; ignoring them can only make your job harder without any benefit to the client.

(c) *Use such aids as are available.* Two or three generations ago it might have been considered lazy to do things the easy way; but what our ancestors then regarded as laziness is now known as efficiency. The pocket calculator is probably the simplest example of an electronic aid, and it should be used in preference to pen-and-ink workings or a slide rule. And if the client's computer and operator are available to you and can be of help, their assistance should not be refused. The client will not wish to pay you a consultancy fee for months of work which the computer could have achieved while you were at lunch.

(d) *But not all time-savers are electronic.* If your consultancy operations require, say, the same calculations to be done again and again, then you should try to devise some kind of tabulation or ready reckoner to which you can refer or, where appropriate, some mathematical constant which you can use repeatedly. If you are often asked to explain the same abstruse point, then you should think it through, set down your reasoning and try to work out a comprehensible way of explaining it, perhaps stage by stage. Maybe you can prepare a booklet or leaflet about it; if you do so you should ensure that your name, address and telephone number are clearly given. Large consultancy firms have substantial stocks of pre-digested material which obviates the need for repetitive thinking. In this way they reap the benefit of the scale of their operations.

(e) *Sometimes it helps to prepare a diagram.* Obviously the diagram must be suited to the problem and to the user's way of thinking, with the reservation that if you are a muddled thinker, you will derive no assistance from a muddled diagram. You need something which will keep your mind clear, not cause further confusion. If the problem is complex, perhaps it can be broken down into its component sub-problems and solved in stages. If so, the diagram can take the form of a tree. This helps to clear the mind about the order in which the sub-problems are to be tackled. If this method is used, it is a good idea not to start work on any stage until the work on all earlier stages has been completed. It is also a good idea to keep the number of possibilities at any stage as low as possible, ideally to two. A large number of possibilities suggests that the problem might advantageously be broken down further.

(f) *Do not fall into the trap of thinking that, by using time-saving methods, you are losing out.* The reasoning is that these methods result in shorter times spent on assignments and therefore a loss of fees. But this line or thought ignores competition. If you do not run your consultancy in the most efficient way possible, you might as well invite your rivals to take over your business.

(g) *Never forget that the client is in business for profit.* He will not be happy if he is presented with outrageously expensive solutions to his problems.

(h) *A consultant is paid to think.* From which it follows that he is entitled to charge for thinking and calculating time so long as it relates to the solution of the client's problems and falls within the terms of his remit. In practice it is not unusual for inspiration to come quite suddenly, perhaps in the bath, in the local or on the golf course. The point here is that, although this off-duty thinking actually happens, the client is not entitled to expect his problems to be solved 'off the clock' and must be prepared to be charged for working time reasonably spent in using your brain.

(j) *Sometimes you need to co-operate.* If you are engaged to work with experts in other fields to solve problems which are not confined to a single discipline — for instance, design consultant with management accountant or metallurgist with engineer — co-operation will be necessary in identifying, and preferably documenting, the problems and the respective roles of the experts. Sometimes, of course, consultants may be working under the same organisation, perhaps as employees or sub-contractors of a large consultancy, in which case their functions will have been clearly defined, but in other cases they may have been hired separately by the client, so that the consultants themselves will need to work out the best way to ensure that their skills are used to advantage, the aim being to avoid duplication of effort due to overlapping.

COMPANY ACCOUNTS — THE HIDDEN SNAGS

We know that companies are in business to make money and that if their managements call in consultants they normally expect improvements in profitability. So it is hardly surprising that, sooner or later, consultants working in the world of business are called upon to study company accounts. The subject is a troublesome one and therefore merits a major section to itself.

The tax man in mind

Given that a company has engaged your consultancy services and expects an improvement, how will that improvement be measured? By looking at the profit figures, of course. And where will the management find the profit figures? In the accounts, obviously. And will they show the improvements which as the consultant you have worked long and hard to achieve? Probably not.

The background to this problem is that company accounts are usually drawn up by financial accountants, and not surprisingly they place strong emphasis on the financial aspects of accounting, an emphasis which is reflected in accounting software and even in the attitudes of some management accountants. The accounts are normally prepared with tax considerations in mind, and so long as they provide the Inspector of Taxes with an acceptable basis for assessing tax he is not remotely concerned with the question whether they are useful to managements and their advisers. And often they are not.

The accounting systems on which company accounts are based were developed in the early years of the twentieth century. Major changes have swept through the business world in the meantime, and in some cases the systems have not been suitably adapted to reflect these. From your consultancy viewpoint the major shortcomings embodied in these systems include faulty allocation of costs among departments, cutting back on discretionary expenditure, and the combining of departmental figures.

Faulty allocation of costs among departments

(For 'departments' wherever it appears please substitute 'products' or 'cost centres' as the context may require.) In other days the main cost item which businesses had to bear was direct labour, a cost which was easy to allocate among departments. For convenience rather than accuracy other costs were allocated in proportion to direct labour, a system which may have worked adequately in the distant past but is almost certain to be unsuitable now. Yet in many cases it has remained in use, regardless of the fact that much of the direct labour has been replaced by machines. From your angle as a consultant this means that you cannot rely on the accounts to give you a realistic idea of the costs of the department on which you are working. If the company's accountants cannot help in this area you may have to work out figures for yourself or, in the last resort, tell the client that no reliable cost figures for the department are available.

Cutting back on discretionary expenditure

Sensible expenditure keeps a company afloat and its business in good shape. But all expenditure, sensible or otherwise, reduces surpluses, and this fact causes managements with a limited outlook to defer expenditure in order to boost accounting profits in the short term. The accounts will show a larger surplus due to cutting back on such items as welfare and customer relations but will not reflect the long-term damage which this policy has caused to the business. And they will certainly not show the ground lost to rivals. You will need to rely on your own observations rather than on the accounts.

Combining of departmental figures

You may well find that the dramatic improvement which you have achieved in a particular department has not received recognition in the accounts. Even assuming that the departmental figures are reliable, which they may not be for the reasons already given, the department which you have pulled up by the bootlaces may have been combined, for accounting purposes, with other departments which have stood still or slipped back. Stock reductions and improvements in quality control and other systems may thus have been submerged.

Company accounts are not sacrosanct

The blame for these shortcomings cannot be laid entirely at the door of the accountants; indeed, the main responsibility lies with managements for failing to insist on accounts which are designed to enable them to manage rather than to get the taxman off their backs. But the message to the consultant is clear: do not regard company accounts as sacrosanct. They probably give a reasonably good idea of the size of the business, but beyond that they may provide little information which will help you with your work. You must be prepared to ask questions to get at the truth, and if you are wise you will make sure that the company management know what you are doing in this respect and why you are doing it.

If you yourself are versed in accounting matters you may feel justified in advising the management to review its systems to ensure that they provide the sort of information which present-day management needs if it is to make good decisions. If you are not an accountant you may think it worthwhile to suggest to the client that they approach their professional accountants on this subject and try to convince them (if indeed they need convincing) that the role of the accountant is not purely historical.

Your advice may not be well received. The management may be content to get by with traditional accounting and to leave its accountants and its software (on which it may have incurred considerable expense) undisturbed.

FEES: FIXING THE RATE FOR THE JOB

In your early days in business as a consultant you will probably be strongly tempted to work without payment, or for an absurdly low fee, in order to get yourself known. The decision whether you should do this must be yours alone, but there is a tendency for clients who have been receiving cut-price service to be very unhappy when expected to pay the full fees. On balance it is better to establish at the outset a policy of charging what the services are worth. But how do you as a newcomer know what you are worth?

The law of the marketplace

If you have time to plan you should try to find out the rates currently being charged for services comparable with your own. Perhaps if you have always been accustomed to salaried or wage-earning employment — maybe on the basis of some well-recognised scale — you will expect to be able to arrive at your fee rate by an established formula. This is not feasible; in self-employment your services are worth what people are prepared to pay for them. The law of the marketplace applies. And the best way to find out what people are likely to pay is to get to know what they are paying already for the nearest equivalent.

In the last resort, however, you may be reduced to trial and error in fixing your first rate. This is not very satisfactory, because erring on the high side is likely to result in loss of business (by pricing yourself out of the market) while erring on the low side means that you will be underpaid for services rendered. For want of any better guide you might consider relating your worth to the salary or wages received before giving up paid employment. Of course, adjustments will have to be made for other benefits of that employment (e.g. National Insurance and pension contributions) and for the fact that, when working for yourself, you will need to cover the expenses of your business. These could be high if you need, say, a workplace, a car and paid assistance. Travelling — apart from that which is done on behalf of, and at the expense of, the client — can be a costly item. So can advertising. And even if you intend working from home, without employees, you will still need time to run your business — to keep records, sell your services, send out fee invoices, make decisions — so you will not be able to spend the whole of every working day earning fees.

All these are factors to be taken into account in arriving at the rate on which your fees will be based. If it is management consultancy, or some other type of work requiring numeracy, which you propose to practise, you may well be able to apply all the factors yourself. If not, you may need to seek help from an accountant. It will be worth your while taking the trouble to find a good accountant who may, with luck, be able to introduce some business.

Quoting and invoicing

Once the fee rate has been settled, you should quote it with confidence and without hesitation. In discussing services with a prospective client his confidence should be gained, if possible, before fees are quoted. (There is nothing sinister about this; a client will be more willing to pay good fees to someone in whom he has confidence than to someone whose trustworthiness is in doubt.) But if the client asks about fees before that stage is reached, you should quote immediately. You will find that some people dislike paying for services because, unlike goods, they cannot be seen or handled. So if a lump sum is quoted to cover the whole job the quotation should be detailed and informative.

Management consultants usually invoice their fees monthly unless the client prefers some other arrangement. Different practices may prevail in other types of consultancy but the main consideration is to suit the convenience of the client.

When a fee invoice is compiled it should show clearly what the fees are for. Expenses should be shown separately. If direct disbursements have been made on behalf of the client — such as buying a new ribbon for his typewriter — these should also be shown separately. Your fees will, of course, include a charge for advice given but not taken. But from a client's viewpoint invoices will not be welcome if there is nothing to show for them. Any fee will seem too high if he is dissatisfied. So in the early days — before a breakthrough has been achieved in solving the client's problem — it is specially important to word the invoices explicitly, so that the client will be in no doubt about the services rendered and their exact costs.

Avoid overcharging — which can take many forms. One is treating overheads as expenses and charging them out as such to clients. This is wrong; the fees should cover them. Another is charging abnormally high fees when a client is in trouble and needs urgent help. And it is not necessarily a good idea to put fees up during an assignment — unless it is a very long one — even if the right to do so has been reserved. Practices of this kind may bring in extra cash in the short term, but they may do lasting damage to client goodwill.

Stick to your quote

Various problems are liable to arise over fees. Some clients will try to avoid paying. 'I could have done this myself!' is a favourite expression. It is usually untrue; in some cases it is possible that, having observed what the consultant has done, the client might make a successful attempt to do it himself next time, but really this aspect of the matter is quite irrelevant. The 'could have done it myself' argument is invalid; having engaged a consultant to do the job the client must pay for it whether he could have done it himself or not. And even if he had done it himself he would have paid for it in the form of use of his own (presumably valuable) time.

If fees can be justified it is unwise, having invoiced them, to cut or waive them; it creates a very bad precedent to do so. Barter is another practice which cannot be recommended. If the client wants you to accept, instead of fees, items which he reckons you can sell profitably to other clients, you will be unwise to agree. Your relations with other clients are no business of the bartering client, who could well be trying to get rid of unsaleable goods. On the other hand, if you genuinely wish to buy a very attractive tea service which your china-shop client has for sale, then let both the consultancy fees and the tea service be properly invoiced; and if all that changes hands is a balancing cheque no harm will be done so long as the correct book entries are made. And neither party need feel under any continuing obligation to the other.

Contingency fees and retainers

A question which, sooner or later, is likely to occupy your mind as a consultant is whether you should charge contingency fees. These are fees of the type envisaged in the expression 'no cure no pay' and the basic arrangement is that if you are successful you will receive a handsome fee, but if you fail you will get nothing. There are, of course, variations on this basic theme, but the general idea is that all or part of the fees will remain 'iffy' until the pre-agreed conditions for payment have been successfully met. Frankly, this is not a good method of charging. Normal fees should provide sufficient motivation, bearing in mind that you are under a duty to do your best for your client anyway, and if you make a practice of relying on contingency fees you may have a run of failures which will extinguish not only your reputation for business professionalism but perhaps also the financial stability of your business itself.

However, no doubt there will always be consultants who, attracted by the possibility of high rewards, will disregard this advice. Perhaps they would rather gamble on fees than on horses. In that case they will need to be sure that the conditions for payment are very clearly drawn up; otherwise loopholes in the arrangements may defeat them.

Some clients prefer to have consultants on retainer; they pay a fixed monthly or yearly fee and are then entitled to seek the consultant's advice, and possibly other services, as required. This obviously provides the consultant with a regular income, but it also places him under a continuing obligation which may hamper his acceptance of other work. If you enter into such an agreement, the services which you can be called upon to provide, and the number of hours which you can be required to work, should be clearly defined, as otherwise a great deal of time may be spent in working for little reward. Remember — clients are not likely to suggest a retainer unless they think it will benefit them.

Time equals money

In some cases a period of notice to end a consultancy assignment (e.g. 28 days on either side) is written into the arrangements. In other cases, especially for short assignments, this is neither necessary nor desirable. Often the assignment can be ended by either party without notice. This is not necessarily as unsatisfactory as it might seem. A consultant who values his reputation is hardly likely to leave unfinished a job for which he has been hired unless the client changes his mind which, of course, may happen if the client considers that the fees are mounting up too quickly. But would a period of notice (during which the parties might well be at variance) be beneficial in any way?

Sometimes you may consider asking for a deposit on account of your fees. In this you must be guided by circumstances. If you have no good reason to think that the client is a bad payer it may be politic to take the risk rather than give offence. On the other hand, if you know that the client is a bad payer, whom you are prepared to lose, then to ask for a deposit is not unreasonable.

You should never charge for time which you yourself have wasted. This may seem obvious, but it is not always so in practice. Let us suppose, for instance, that you will have to delay proceeding with an assignment because necessary information has not yet come to hand. If the delay in its arrival is due to your own failure to get it, or to make a timely request for it, you will be very unwise to try to charge the client for the time thus wasted.

Finally, long credit should not be allowed. If a monthly invoice is still outstanding when the next one is rendered, you should at least consider suspending the work until payment is made. This is subject, of course, to any arrangement which you may have made with the client and to any special circumstances which may apply in a particular case, such as the illness of the person who has to approve your accounts for payment. But generally speaking a lax payer is liable to become even more lax if he is not placed under any pressure.

PART TWO
OPERATING A PROFITABLE CONSULTANCY

GOOD MANAGEMENT — THE KEY TO SUCCESS

It has already been stressed that consultancy is a business. Like any other business it needs to be competently managed if it is to stand a reasonable chance of success. Profitability will depend heavily on making the best possible use of your time as a consultant; it must not be wasted on activities which make no contribution to the prosperity of the business. You must never forget that consultancy time is what the business has to sell and that proper records of its use must be kept. Slackness in keeping these adequately (they're so boring!) could result in serious financial loss and perhaps failure. But there is more — much more — to running a successful consultancy than just keeping records of what has already happened — historical records, to use a convenient term.

The family angle

Many businesses fail quite soon after starting. Some collapse due to bad luck, but many more founder due to inadequate management. And there are personal and family aspects to be taken into account. It is essential that a person starting up a consultancy should have the support of his family if he has one. This does not mean that they must all work in the business alongside him, but it does mean that they must accept that he has gone into business to make a success of it and that they must be prepared to help when they can and avoid placing obstacles in his way.

In many cases, of course, couples work happily together in running a business and so do parents and children, but it is impossible to generalise on whether it is desirable for members of a family to work in a business together as this depends to a large extent on individual personalities and aptitudes. In theory, suitability should be the overriding factor in choosing a business partner or employee, but it has to be accepted that availability often assumes greater importance, especially in a one-man business, where it may be better to have the telephone answered by a member of your family than to entrust that task to an answering machine.

Anticipating your and your clients' needs

What do the clients want? Having regard to changing conditions, will their requirements still be the same next year? Or five or ten years hence? A well-managed consultancy that can anticipate need and be ready to meet it stands a far better chance of survival than one which remains inert until it is faced with an urgent need to reappraise what the business has to offer. What applies to manufacturing and retailing applies equally to consultancy as well: You cannot be sure that the same skill and knowledge will remain marketable at consultancy level throughout your business life.

As a fledgling consultant you will need to be as sure as you can that you are the right person to be in charge of a new venture. Maybe you have answered the questions in the section 'what is a consultant' to your own satisfaction, but only time will tell whether you really have the drive and energy — and, indeed, the health — to work hard, withstand competition, exploit your skills and personality and (though perhaps not immediately) derive a reasonable income from the enterprise.

But for the moment let us assume that you are successful. Who will inherit and run your business? You will not live forever, but perhaps the business is of so personal a type that it will die with you. Otherwise as a prudent consultant you will make arrangements for it to continue. You will make a will. Moreover, you will have it prepared by a competent draftsman who understands business problems and can advise on the best way of preventing the family resources from being unduly depleted by taxation.

Has the small business had its day?

This is a question which arouses many emotions. The small grocer used to give good personal service. But now he has virtually disappeared, and so have many others like him. But emotions cannot be the basis for a satisfactory answer to the question.

The small grocer became extinct because larger businesses were able to achieve economies of scale which were not open to him. And economies of scale can apply to services as well as to goods. In other days a solicitor could set himself up in practice with little more than a desk, typewriter and telephone. In theory this would still be possible but unless he was a specialist unique in his area he would find himself in competition with other solicitors who, by using computers, word processors and other equipment, were able to achieve a much greater output than he could.

But there are still areas in which economies of scale do not operate. Some work must still be done individually, whether in a large or a small organisation; and work which does not require elaborate equipment of a type which would be under-used in a small concern still leaves scope for the exercise of a consultant's skills on an economic and, hopefully, profitable basis. So in running your consultancy you need to think and plan and to avoid areas in which you are bound to be undersold. You must concentrate on giving excellent personal service. And if a change of course is necessary you will probably find that you are better able to adapt than is a large organisation with substantial investments which are based on the expectation of maintaining the *status quo*. All the advantages of smallness must be understood and exploited.

YOUR CONSULTANCY BUSINESS STRUCTURE

You are faced with a choice when going into business: will you carry it on entirely alone, will you go into partnership with others, or will you form a company? The differences between partnerships and companies are not always clearly understood. A partnership is simply a relationship between people who carry on business together for profit. In England and Wales, unlike Scotland, a partnership is not a separate entity, distinct from the persons who comprise it. But a company *is* a separate entity; it is a legal 'person' and can own assets and owe money just like a living person. Most companies are 'limited by shares' which means that the members own shares in the company. They do not own the company's assets (the company does) and they do not owe its debts (again, the company does). All the three main types of business structure have advantages and disadvantages, as you will discover.

Individual alone ('sole trader')

Among the advantages, a sole trader owns all the assets and takes all the profits of the business. So long as he complies with the law he has complete freedom to run the business as he wishes. His Class 2 National Insurance contributions are low when compared with the amounts which an employer and employee together would pay, though his National Insurance position is more complicated than this, as we shall see later. He is permitted to make substantial payments out of income to provide a pension for himself and he can claim tax relief on them. And finally, but very importantly, no one except himself and the Inland Revenue, and perhaps any other government departments concerned with his affairs, need see his accounts or know how much he earns. This information is not available for public inspection.

Turning to the disadvantages, the sole trader is personally responsible for the debts of the business which means, to take an extreme case, that he can be forced to sell his house to meet them. If the business loses money the loss falls entirely on him and if it makes money he pays income tax on the entire profit, even if he leaves it in the business. But he can, in general, offset losses against profits for tax purposes. As regards National Insurance, although, as we have mentioned, the Class 2 contributions are relatively low, the benefits are also restricted. In particular the self-employed person does not qualify for unemployment benefit. And he will probably be liable for Class 4 National Insurance contributions which, despite their name, are a form of tax bringing no benefits whatever.

Forming a partnership

A partnership is legally defined as 'the relation which subsists between persons carrying on business in common with a view of profit'. A partnership may exist quite informally, without a written agreement, but in such a case it is entirely governed by legal rules. These rules, which may be at variance with the partners' wishes, are fairly rigid, and it is a false economy to dispense with a professionally-drawn agreement.

To avoid confusion it needs to be made clear that partnership is not the same thing as co-ownership. It is possible for co-owners of business premises and equipment to share facilities and staff and yet not be partners. Barristers and medical practitioners, usually in consultant rather than general practice, afford good examples of this. Each practitioner has his own individual practice and keeps separate accounts. The system requires clearly defined arrangements as well as tact, loyalty and understanding. It appears to work satisfactorily within the professions, where rules of professional conduct and etiquette apply, but one would hesitate to recommend it for more general business use. It is not difficult to share premises if each co-owner has his own room but it can be extremely difficult to share staff if all the co-owners are busy.

The advantages of partnership are very similar to those of sole trading. The partners together own the assets subject to any agreement between them. (It is not unusual for a sole trader, taking others into partnership, to continue to own the business premises and lease them to the new firm.) They share the profits as agreed and, like sole traders, they pay Class 2 National Insurance contributions. And again their accounts are not open to the public, though of course each partner knows the income which the others derive from the business.

The disadvantages of a partnership are also very similar to those of sole trading. Losses fall on the partners with the right to offset certain losses against taxable profits. The rules regarding income tax and National Insurance are those which apply to sole traders. But two important points should be borne in mind. Firstly, a partner, unlike a sole trader, has to be prepared to reconcile his views with those of other people (his partners) if the venture is not to break up in disarray. Secondly, any partner who has the necessary resources may have to bear the whole of the firm's liabilities if the other partners are impecunious. To put it another way, one can be ruined by one's partners. There is an exception to this; it is possible to set up a 'limited partnership' in which one or some of the partners cannot be made liable beyond a certain limit. This arrangement is seldom used since it is not very satisfactory to have unlimited partners shouldering the burden. Another point which should be borne in mind, though it cannot be readily classified as an advantage or disadvantage, is that on a change in the partnership — when new partners join or existing ones leave — the consequences need to be carefully thought out or money may be lost. It is an area in which expert tax advice should be sought.

Establishing a company

This is the most expensive option, at all events in the early stages, as it involves forming a company or, if time is short, buying a ready-formed 'shelf' company and perhaps changing its name.

It is well established that a company is a separate legal 'person' distinct from the individuals who own it (members) and run it (directors). Put very simply, the people who form or buy a company put money into it (share capital) and receive shares in exchange. The company then has capital for running its business. In the case of a limited company, the members are not liable to pay any money into the company beyond the amounts, if any, unpaid for their shares. Nor are they liable to pay the debts of the company, for the obvious reason that the company, as a separate person, must pay them out of its own resources. That, at all events, is the theoretical position. The reality is often different. People who have dealings with a company, and especially those who provide it with finance, such as banks, are well aware of the implications of limited liability and often insist, as a condition of providing finance, that individuals (directors or members) shall give personal guarantees of the company's debts, which means that they may still lose their houses if the business fails. In this way limited liability — one of the main reasons for using a company — is often thrown away before the company even starts business.

But quite apart from limited liability there may be other advantages of using a company. Directors and staff are employees of the company; they pay tax under PAYE and their salaries are deducted from the company's profits before the company, if liable, is charged with corporation tax. And profits may be left in the business without having to pay high income tax on them, an option not available to sole traders or partners. Various tax exemptions and reliefs may be available, and this again is an area in which competent advice is essential if money is not to be lost.

Another such area, in a small company in which the members and directors are the same persons, is centred on the question of how much should be paid out as salaries (to the directors) and how much as dividends (to the same persons as members). Tax is treated as having been deducted from dividends before they reach the members. But all the tax implications, not just some of them, need to be taken into account, and there is often considerable scope for optimisation by a knowledgeable person. Further information about tax is to be found later in the section 'Planning your tax payments' but before leaving the subject for the time being it should be pointed out that among the eventual advantages of using a company, perhaps not relevant in the early days, is the possibility of benefits from company-operated pension schemes and employee share schemes. There may also be scope for saving Inheritance Tax.

Among the disadvantages of using a company, apart from the expense of forming it, is the fact that the members cannot offset the company's losses for the purpose of mitigating their own personal income tax. And there are higher National Insurance contributions to be met, though the benefits are more comprehensive. But the greatest disadvantage is probably the need for limited companies to file audited annual accounts which the public can inspect. Rivals can thus get some idea of the size and nature of the business. And, of course, the preparation and audit of the accounts can be a costly business, though the requirements for small companies are not as stringent as those for larger ones. This disadvantage — having to file accounts which the public can see — can be overcome, albeit with the loss of limited liability, by using an unlimited company. This may be quite suitable for consultants who do not expect to incur large debts. This type of company, though less usual than limited ones, is still a legal person, a separate entity, and is treated as such for tax purposes.

Making up your mind

If as a consultant you do not expect to have large financial commitments, or to need expensive staff, you will probably be able to operate very well as a sole trader. But as your business expands you should seek advice. To buy a 'shelf' company without guidance and without any previous experience of company matters is unwise; but far worse is to buy, or buy into, an existing trading company without proper investigations. Indeed, the whole subject of buying an existing consultancy — whether a company or not — bristles with complications and merits a whole section to itself.

TAKING OVER AN EXISTING CONSULTANCY

For the newcomer to the world of consultancy buying an existing consultancy, or a large interest in one, may seem to be an excellent way of getting off to a flying start. And so it is, if the price is right and all the conditions are ideal. But often they are not. Indeed, a transaction of this kind is full of pitfalls for the unwary.

What are you buying?

If the business is unincorporated (i.e. not run as a company) the price is likely to include premises, goodwill, equipment and stock, or a share in these if the newcomer is buying in as a partner. If he is buying outright he will not normally accept responsibility for the ex-owner's debts, but if for some exceptional reason he does, this should be allowed for in the price. If he is buying in as a partner, the existing debts of the partnership will be one of the items to be taken into account in the negotiations. The same principle applies: if the partnership share is to be burdened with debt it will not be worth as much as if it were unencumbered.

But what about the assets; do the sellers really own what they are proposing to sell? Are some of the assets, or apparent assets, on hire, or hire purchase, or mortgaged? Is the stock (if any) of any use? And as for goodwill, this can only have a value to the incomer if he is acceptable to the existing clientele. These are but a few of the possible snags.

Lurking dangers

If the business is a company the transaction will consist of a sale of shares in it. And here the danger of losing one's money is even greater. All the problems mentioned above must be guarded against, but there is another danger inherent in the very nature of a company, which is that it may have liabilities lurking in the background. As we have seen, a company is a legal person. It continues to be the same person whoever owns its shares. So let us suppose that when the company's last annual accounts were prepared they showed a healthy profit, with a strong balance sheet. It is on the strength of these accounts that the newcomer is prepared to buy the shares. And let us further suppose that, since the date to which the accounts were made up, the Inland Revenue have indicated that the company is under investigation for alleged tax frauds. If the allegations were substantiated the company could be driven into insolvency and liquidation. The sellers of the shares (very nice people, no doubt!) have said nothing about this activity on the part of the Revenue. The buyer remains in blissful ignorance of it and thinks he is on to a good buy. Once he has taken over the ownership of the shares he learns of the tax claim. The company has the option of settling it or fighting (and perhaps losing) a very expensive legal battle. The very agreeable ex-owners — the only people who might be able to provide the information necessary for opposing the tax claim — can no longer be traced. The buyer has been swindled.

Safeguarding your interests

From what has been said, as an intending buyer you might conclude that you should not touch an existing consultancy business with a bargepole. But that, of course, might mean losing a genuinely good purchase. Therefore, you should employ an excellent solicitor and accountant, each of them well versed in commercial transactions. The accountant will study the accounts and make such enquiries as he thinks necessary about tax and other liabilities and potential liabilities. The solicitor will study the vending agreement and make sure that it contains all the warranties, undertakings and indemnities which you will need. If and and when the documents are in order the two advisers, working in co-operation with each other, will advise you that it is safe to go ahead.

ARRANGING YOUR FINANCE

If you intend to run your consultancy from home and work locally you may not need much finance. By contrast, if your business requires a laboratory and an office, and you expect to travel internationally, then you will require suitable sources of funds if you do not possess the liquid resources yourself. In any case, quite apart from equipment and premises, the running expenses of the business will have to be met, and those who are to depend upon it will have to live, until a good fee income starts to come in.

Looking for loans

Some businesses are fortunate enough to qualify for grants and loans from central government or local bodies. But where no possibility of tapping these sources exists it is necessary to look to conventional ones. In general, finance for more than ten years is regarded as long term; under three years, short term; and in between, medium term. So, you should be clear about the period for which you will require the facility. And, of course, you must work out how much you will need. In doing this you should allow for contingencies and for possible spending in the early days when you are creating an image.

Looking at it from the point of view of the organisations or individuals who will provide the finance, the risk will have to be evaluated. They will weigh the possibility of things going wrong — not only outright failure but difficulties with cash flow and profitability. On the basis of their assessment they will decide on the rate of interest and the security which they require. As the applicant you will normally be expected to bring in funds yourself as your own stake in the business.

When starting your consultancy, of the different forms of finance that may be available to you, you must decide which will best suit your needs. The following brief description of the more usual types will help you to make up your mind.

Short-term finance

This, in practice, probably means an overdraft or short-term loan from a local bank and perhaps, if equipment is required, hire-purchase or leasing. Other forms of short-term finance exist, such as factoring and discounting, but they are more expensive, and in any case they are better suited to sellers of goods than to providers of services, and especially providers of personal and confidential services. The existence of a third party, such as a factor or the drawee of a bill of exchange, might cause the consultant's clients considerable disquiet.

Bank borrowing can often be quickly arranged, and in the case of an overdraft the interest is charged on a day-to-day basis on the amount overdrawn. This interest is usually debited quarterly, and the customer's credit rating is a major factor in fixing the rate of interest, which is variable. Loans are less flexible than overdrafts; interest is charged on the full amount of a loan until it is repaid. An overdraft is repayable on demand, though in practice it is seldom called without reasonable notice. Banks do not normally interfere in the running of a business unless, in the case of a company, they appoint a receiver.

Hire-purchase involves hiring an asset and paying regular instalments. The asset continues to be owned by the seller (or finance house) until, at the end of the agreed payment period, the hirer can opt to acquire the asset as his own. Leasing is a way of acquiring the *use* of an asset without the ownership, though some leasing arrangements do include an option to purchase.

Medium- and long-term finance

It is unlikely that a normal small consultancy practice will require finance on a medium- or long-term basis, though everyone in practice on his own account may find some knowledge of the subject useful if only to be able to discuss it sensibly with clients and their financial advisers.

A concern wishing to purchase fixed assets (buildings, plant, machinery) or seeking to expand its business may need funds for periods longer than short-term lenders are prepared to allow. In some instances a business may qualify for a government guarantee and so obtain a loan which would not otherwise be available to it.

Long-term finance may be forthcoming from banks, venture capital funds, other types of fund, or individuals. Each arrangement will be worked out to meet the particular circumstances and should be properly documented. If the finance takes the form of a loan the interest may be charged at a rate above the prevailing market rate, and there may be penalties for repayment before a prescribed date. But in many cases the lender may require an equity holding — a share in the business — as one of the conditions of providing finance and this, of course, will reduce the owner's interest in the business. Investors tend to back people rather than products; but they expect the people to have something more than marvellous ideas. The ideas must have applications which will make money.

Applying for finance

When you approach a bank or other lender or investor it is important for you to ensure that the application is presented in the best possible way to show that the proposal is feasible and to gain the confidence of the lender or investor. If you are in any doubt about your ability to put it together satisfactorily you should approach your accountant for help. In particular the financier will want to know:

(a) how much money is wanted (the larger the amount the more detail will be required);
(b) what it is to be used for, allowing for contingencies;
(c) how much you will put in yourself (your stake);
(d) the quality of management (i.e. how good you are reckoned to be at running a business);
(e) the level of risk;
(f) all aspects of the project which are relevant to its viability;
(g) whether all the aspects have been properly thought through;
(h) when (if at all) repayment is to be expected (it will not be expected so far as a permanent investment is in contemplation); and
(i) what security is being offered.

It will be helpful to provide a cash flow forecast; a business may be profitable on paper yet fail due to having no money available when needed. And the effects of taxation should not be overlooked when preparing the information. If the application is being made to a bank, you should not expect it to accept high risks. Other sources may accept such risks, but the greater the risk the more likely it is that a stake in the equity (a shareholding) will be required. And the larger the stake the greater the risk that the investor will become a virtual employer.

Avoid friends and relatives — if possible

No treatment of the subject of finance would be complete without a brief mention of the possibility of seeking loans and investments from friends and relatives. It is pointless to say that this should be avoided at all costs since it may be the only source of finance available to you. If this source is used, it is particularly important to document the arrangements properly, otherwise unpleasant misunderstandings may arise. And sometimes the line of demarcation between credit and theft can become very blurred. It will do your reputation no good to be thought to have strayed on to the wrong side of that line.

SETTING UP YOUR OWN PREMISES

When you need an office, workshop or laboratory, and cannot work at home or on clients' premises, you will be faced with the need to buy, lease or rent suitable property. Leasing and renting are similar in that they entail buying the use of premises belonging to someone else. A lease, however, may require the payment of a lump sum (a premium) as well as rent, and the parties will be bound for a fixed period, whereas renting on a periodic tenancy does not normally involve a premium and the parties' obligations are usually less onerous than those applicable to leases. If you rent premises you do not tie up capital or have any problems about raising funds for purchase, but on the other hand you have no inducement to improve premises which are not your own and you will be unable to include ownership of the premises as an asset if you decide to sell your business.

Seek professional advice

A property deal of any kind, whether buying, leasing or renting, calls for caution, and a sensible consultant will seek advice from a solicitor and a surveyor. We have not yet reached a stage at which a single firm can provide the services of both, though events are moving in that direction. Once he is in occupation under a lease or tenancy a business occupier may by law have some security against being turned out, even when the agreed term has expired, but this is a matter which depends on changeable legislation and should be checked when necessary.

Another relevant factor is town and country planning. Controls are not confined to restricting what may be erected, such as hoardings or unsightly buildings in beauty spots. They also affect the use to which premises may be put. For instance, if the owner of a house in a desirable residential area starts using it for the manufacture of fish glue, the complaints from other residents will soon result in his being ordered to stop, even though he may have made no outwardly visible change to his house. That is an extreme case, used to illustrate the nature of the control, but a borderline case can be even more troublesome if it entails long and possibly expensive wrangling with the authorities about the uses to which the occupier may put his premises.

Location, space, and running costs

Location may also be important, but probably not as much so to a consultant as it would be to, say, a retailer needing to be on a prime site. Obviously your premises should be accessible to clients if they need to call. And generally you and your employees, if any, should be able to work in peace and concentrate on the job. Usually this is not a difficult requirement to meet; it is surprisingly easy to accustom yourself to express trains rushing past the window. You soon cease to notice them — though this would not apply to visitors or temporary employees.

Space for possible expansion is another consideration, though again probably not as important for a consultancy as it would be for other types of business. It is generally easier to uproot a consultancy than to move a manufacturing operation. Services such as water, gas, electricity and telephone will no doubt be essential, but a consultancy seldom needs unusual services such as a hydraulic main or a pipeline carrying argon.

Running costs are vitally important. It would be the height of folly to cripple a new business with excessive rent, rates, lighting, heating and insurance. And are any grants or concessions available? Probably not but it does no harm to enquire.

Equipment and stock

This is a subject on which it is impossible to generalise as the needs of different types of consultancy work vary so widely. A telephone and typewriter, with a small stock of letter paper and other stationery, may suffice for the consultant who intends to work mainly at his clients' premises and who can use a good reference library when necessary. But if you have to solve problems in your own laboratory or workshop, you may need a great deal of expensive equipment. How should you choose it?

First of all you should try to foresee the type of problem which you are most likely to be called upon to solve. A specialist, by definition, is not expected to be an expert in everything or to range over a very wide field. He must view his skills narrowly, define the areas within which he stands out as an expert, and equip accordingly. Therefore, until you are fully established you should consider whether you can meet your clients' requirements without enormous outlay, perhaps — if it can be done without giving away clients' secret processes or know-how — by using someone else's facilities on an agreed basis of payment. Once you are established you can talk to your clients and get a better idea of their likely requirements. Problems are there to be solved, and if as a budding consultant you cannot solve your own you are unlikely to gain your clients' confidence in solving theirs. Many a successful business has been built on a shoestring, and you must use your imagination in getting suitably equipped.

Stock control

Stock is a matter with which many consultants have little concern, and again it will be the laboratory and workshop users who will face the main problems. In deciding what to stock you will need to think on the same lines as you did with equipment. You will also need to establish — at the outset — a system of stock control so that you will know when to re-order, allowing extra time for items which may be in short supply. Your aim should be to keep sufficient in stock for normal use but avoid overstocking, which ties up valuable capital.

The number of stock control systems in use is almost infinite; some are computer-based, but if the items in stock are not numerous a manual system may be adequate. It is important that, whatever system is used, it should be properly maintained, with stock used being recorded and, where applicable, debited against the client for whom it has been used.

It should be added that a bound book is seldom an effective instrument of stock control. It tends to get untidy and incomprehensible. If a computer is not used a card index may be the best form of control, using a separate card for each distinguishable type of item in stock. You should not attempt to save stationery by using one card for several different items; this is a false economy which could wreck the system.

BECOMING AN EMPLOYER

A person's capacity for work is limited both by the time and energy available for business and by the bounds of his or her own abilities. If your consultancy expands, the time will come when you will have to consider your future plans. Will you take on employees? Will you sub-contract some of the work? Or will you turn business away? Some readers will be horrified by the last suggestion, but many businesses acquire a fringe of unprofitable work as time goes on and shedding this might, provided it can be done without giving offence to valued clients, solve the problem for the time being.

To employ or not to employ?

The question will no doubt have to be faced, sooner or later, whether the circumstances, viewed as a whole and taking alternatives into account, justify the engagement of employees. If the answer is yes, will they be full-time or part-time? Temporary or permanent? If you work alone you will not usually need a large staff, and even a full-time secretary may be under-employed. However, answering the telephone may present a problem, especially if you are frequently away on assignments. One possibility is an answering machine — but some callers dislike these. Another solution is a portable telephone which will enable callers to reach you wherever you are — but this may result in a call coming through during an important meeting with another client. A further possibility, which again will cause horror in some circles, is to leave the telephone unanswered while you are away. This may not be as unsatisfactory as it seems and if the possibility of being telephoned is remote you may feel that the risk is worth taking. And it probably does less harm than receiving a call and failing to act on it.

Staff involve expenses beyond their salaries. For instance, National Insurance, pensions, training, welfare, health and safety, sickness payments and perhaps redundancy must all be taken into account, quite apart from the need to provide a workplace. Other factors which may come into reckoning are trade union pressures, discrimination (race and sex), women's maternity pay and leave, length of notice to dismiss, and rights of employees when a business changes hands.

Picking the right person

Having decided to engage someone, you must get and keep your mind clear about what the job is. What will its title be? What will be the objective, the functions, the duties and responsibilities? These considerations should be properly worked out and set down on paper. If they simply remain in your head it is unlikely that they will assume a sufficiently precise form.

When this has been done you should think about the kind of person who will satisfy the requirements. What educational standards will be necessary? Qualifications? Experience? Age group? Other characteristics? One mistake frequently made in engaging staff is to set too much store by experience as compared with intelligence. In an age of change, and an environment in which every client's problem has to be thought through individually, experience of what happened in the past may actually militate against giving open-minded consideration to what ought to happen now.

When you have decided what sort of person you are looking for, you should try to fix the salary and other benefits to be offered. Unless they are sufficient to attract suitable people against competition it is a waste of time and money to take matters any further. Assuming, however, that the package is right, steps must be taken to find the person. Sometimes this can be done through personal contacts or recommendations. A Jobcentre may be able to provide candidates, but if the vacancy is for a professionally qualified person it may be necessary to approach an agency — perhaps a specialist one — or to advertise. Agencies charge for their services, the fee usually constituting a percentage of the starting salary, but this should be clarified before instructing them. If an advertisement is used it should give a clear and truthful description of what is being offered. Misleading advertisements may result in a number of applications, but the list will soon melt away when the truth emerges. Vague expressions such as 'good salary for the right person' should be avoided. If you want to mention salary at all, you should quote the range you have in mind. And the reference to 'the right person' implies that if the wrong person is engaged he or she must expect a poor salary!

As we have mentioned earlier, it is not always a good idea for relatives to run a business together, and the same applies to the employment of close personal friends. It is quite possible for jealousies to develop into acrimony of a kind which would probably not have occurred had the parties been strangers. It is not pleasant, to say the least, to have to save one's business by booting out, for incompetence, the person who was once one's best friend, and the possibility of having to do this should be thought about before taking him or her on.

Making your decision

All applications should be studied and acknowledged. The interviews will have to be arranged at suitable times and places, bearing in mind that some applicants may not wish their employers to know that they are applying for a new job. That is reasonable; what is not reasonable is for an applicant at interview to launch into a tirade against his present employer. If he does so you will be justified in assuming that, if the applicant is engaged, as his new employer you will likewise be criticised when the time has come for him to move on again. Details of each applicant should be noted before seeing the next one, and comparisons made only when all have been seen. If you are an inexperienced interviewer you should seek professional help.

When a decision has been made an offer should be sent to the successful applicant. It should be sent by letter, which should be precisely drafted, as acceptance of the terms offered will result in a binding contract, and it will then be too late to introduce new terms or to vary existing ones. If, for instance, the offer is subject to references, or a medical check, or early availability, this should be stated. When the offer has been accepted the unsuccessful applicants should be informed that the vacancy has been filled.

As soon as possible after starting work — and certainly within 13 weeks after doing so — the new employee should be given a written statement setting out the terms of employment. This — and the need to update it if changes occur — are legal requirements. The law prescribes what the statement must contain, and printed forms for the purpose can be obtained from commercial stationers. But if the employee has a written service contract which fulfils all the legal requirements, then there is no need to supply a statement as well.

Keeping good employees

Having found good staff, how do you keep them? The blind loyalty which used to bind a 'servant' to his 'master' throughout his working life is a thing of the past, and nowadays an employer has to earn the loyalty of his employees. In the context of a consultancy practice a good employee, engaged on profitable work, can enhance the fee income of the business, and if he does so it is not unreasonable that he should be well treated. In any case, the employee has a number of statutory rights which apply even if they are not referred to in the contract or statement.

But employees have obligations as well as rights, and they must expect their employer to exercise a measure of control. Staff who come into contact with the public must be courteous and discreet, and as their employer you are entitled to expect honesty and reliability at all times. You should clamp down on petty dishonesty: it is the thin end of the wedge. And you should resist any temptation to over-promote a good employee in order to retain their services. If the employee is out of their depth the position is not satisfactory to either party.

Remuneration packages, including differentials, should be kept competitive, based on standards prevailing in the locality, and there should be a regular review taking performance into account. Adequate employment records must be maintained and legal obligations complied with, not forgetting, if computerised employee records are maintained, the Data Protection Act.

Inevitably, as an employer you will find that your staff do not see everything your way; but you should make due allowance for the likelihood that your horizons are much broader than theirs. However, you should avoid adopting a patronising manner towards your staff — this will only alienate them.

Pension schemes

Although it is unlikely that as a consultant in your early days in business you will want to set up a pension scheme for employees, a section about employment would be incomplete without an outline of the subject. Over and above the flat-rate state pensions there is a State Earnings Related Pension Scheme (Serps) which, in return for contributions, provides additional pensions which are related, as the name indicates, to employees' earnings. Employers can, if they wish, contract out of Serps if their own pension schemes provide a satisfactory alternative. Employees may also make their own pension arrangements, which they may find more satisfactory if they are likely to change their employment.

Company schemes usually provide pensions based on final salary, the normal maximum being two-thirds of that salary. They are either insured schemes, in which the benefits are provided by insurance policies written to correspond with the rules of the scheme, or self-administered schemes, in which contributions are invested to provide a fund out of which the benefits are paid. Personal pension arrangements, however, are not based on final salary; they operate on the 'money purchase' principle, under which the size of the pension depends on the amount of money in the fund which has accumulated from invested contributions over the years of membership of the privately arranged scheme.

There are considerable tax advantages in establishing company pension schemes which comply with prescribed requirements. Employers'contributions are treated as a business expense — and therefore allowed against taxable income — and employees' contributions are also allowed against their income taxable under PAYE.

ADMINISTRATION IS A MUST

One certain way of ruining a good business is to neglect the administrative work. Your consultancy may be well marketed and offer a good service, but if its central administration is not functioning it will soon run into difficulties. The clerical work, tedious though it may seem, must be kept up to date.

Record-keeping

A small consultancy does not need elaborate records. However, it does need records. It is not necessary to acquire a computer if the amount of work is insufficient to justify one, but you should establish and maintain (this word is used advisedly) records of:

1. Clients' names, addresses and telephone numbers
2. Prospective clients to be approached
3. Current assignments (there should be a file for each)
4. Completed assignments (files should be retained if they may be needed for reference)
5. Fees invoiced (these should be kept so long as they may be needed for accounting purposes)
6. Fees unpaid
7. Receipts and payments (payments should be recorded under suitable headings for accounting purposes, e.g. stationery, car expenses, postage, etc.)
8. Stocks, if held
9. Cash flow, including a forecast
10. Insurances

11. Employees (including all necessary PAYE, National Insurance, sick pay and pension records)
12. Value Added Tax (if applicable).

Some of these records call for further consideration. It is quite useless, for instance, to keep the names and addresses of clients in some central place, such as an address book, unless they are kept up to date. It would be better to look up the client's most recent address in his file. But then, suppose the file has been destroyed, and you want to tell him about a new service in which he might be interested? The file should *not* have been destroyed while it contained any usable information.

A file for a current assignment should contain details of the time spent and expenses incurred on the job, and again it should be kept right up to date. If you are working on the client's premises it is useful to have the file with you so that you can give the client information about fees and expenses if asked.

Completed assignments

Files for completed assignments should be kept as long as there is a need for them. In particular it may be useful to keep them intact for several weeks or months in case the client raises any queries about the job. When the likelihood of this has passed any papers which belong to the client, or which may be useful to him, should be sent to him (or preferably taken if opportunity offers) so that he will be reminded of your existence. Many a new assignment has resulted from a renewed contact of this kind. Whether the rest of the file is worth keeping depends on what it contains. If it includes information about the client's working practices which may be useful in future assignments for him it should be kept.

Of course any information required for accounting purposes should be retained as long as is necessary. Copies of reports to the client may also be worth keeping; one day a client may deny that he was ever told something vital and the consultant, with the copy report before him, will be able to refute this.

Maintaining systems

Other records may be necessary and other clerical work may have to be done, depending on the nature of the work. Systems should be adequate for their purpose but should not cause unnecessary work. They should be well designed (time spent on designing good systems is usually fully justified) and related to the size of your operation. For instance, a business with 300 debtors needs well-designed records for keeping track of them. But a small consultancy is unlikely to have 300 debtors, and if it has only three a simple list will suffice. Names can be added and deleted as required and amounts can be altered in ink.

A computer is a great asset if there is suitable work for it to do. In particular it can cope with vast amounts of routine work very quickly. But sometimes it is simpler and less time-consuming to do the work manually, aided, perhaps, by an electronic calculator.

Lastly, two important considerations:

1. Whatever filing systems are used they should be capable of expansion to meet the future needs of the business.
2. A consultant who cannot keep books and records properly should engage someone, perhaps a part-timer, to undertake this important aspect of the business.

KEEPING UP WITH LEGISLATION

Every year Parliament enacts a large number of Acts of Parliament, or statutes as they are generally known. Government departments and others produce further legislation under powers delegated to them by the statutes. And every working day the courts are trying to understand the meaning of the legislation, as applied to particular cases, and placing their own interpretations on it.

Everyone is supposed to know the law, yet no one — not even the most learned of lawyers — can really know more than a small fraction of it. However, everyone who is in business needs to try to understand the law so far as it affects him and be ready to seek advice if he thinks he is getting out of his depth.

Here is a brief list of just some of the topics which are covered by legislation and which you will need to understand:

Companies
Company Directors Disqualification
Consumer Credit
Corporation Tax
Data Protection
Employment
Equal Pay
European Communities
Factories
Finance (Acts are passed yearly)
Fire Precautions
Health and Safety at Work
Income Tax
Insolvency
Landlord and Tenant
National Insurance
Offices and Shops
Partnership
Patents, Designs and Marks
Race Relations
Sale of Goods
Sex Discrimination
Social Security
Trade Descriptions
Value Added Tax
Weights and Measures

This is, of course, only a selection, and there may well be other legislation applicable to particular business activities. Most of the titles on the list are self-explanatory and give a good idea of the ground which the legislation covers. But a few need to be explained.

Company Directors Disqualification Act

The duties and responsibilities of company directors are more onerous than they have ever been before. The consequences of failure to fulfil them can be serious and can include disqualification from office as a director. It is very unwise for anyone to accept a directorship without knowing, at least in general terms, what his responsibilities will be and whether he is capable of meeting them. At one time it was common practice to appoint people with no knowledge of business (members of the founder's family, for instance) to seats on the board. Nowadays such a person would be running a considerable personal risk.

Data Protection Act

If employee records (other than mere payroll information) are kept by computer this Act should be studied. The persons to whom the data relates are given certain rights. There is an official known as the Data Protection Registrar, based in Wilmslow, one of whose duties is to guide data users in complying with the requirements.

Employment Acts

These contain numerous requirements affecting the relationship between employer and employee. Over the years there have been many changes, reflecting the policies of the parties in power, and it seems likely that these will continue throughout the foreseeable future.

Landlord and Tenant Act

This Act gives certain rights to those who occupy business premises as tenants. The legislation is complex and should be studied in relation to the facts of each particular case.

European Communities Act

This provides the legal authority under which Britain is a member of the European Community and therefore subject to Community legislation. In these days frontiers are low, and consultants may find that their clients are trading in many lands, both within and without the European Community. Some of the countries may have laws which are very different from those of England, and it is very easy to fall foul of the enactments (some of them politically motivated and perhaps vindictive) of a foreign land. This was discussed in the section 'Problem solving', and the advice given there holds good: seek advice from someone well versed in the laws concerned.

PLANNING YOUR TAX PAYMENTS

As a newly-established consultant you may regard tax as something which can safely be left over to be reckoned with in the rather distant future. After all, you no longer have your income tax deducted under PAYE, all your fees are paid in full, and everything is splendid. So why should you bother to think about tax? A rude awakening will await you if you don't.

Whatever the structure of your consultancy may be, it is important that you should have at least a general acquaintance with tax legislation, if only so that you know when to seek advice. Better decisions can be made if the tax consequences are understood. Good planning can often mitigate a tax burden, whereas taking things as they come may be very expensive.

Income and corporation tax

Sole traders and partners pay income tax on their taxable profits. Rates vary from time to time; taxing statutes are by no means easy to follow, and guidance may be desirable to optimise the position in the early years. Even the choice of annual accounting date may be relevant; a well-chosen date can materially assist cash flow by postponing as long as possible the time when the tax has to be paid.

Companies do not pay income tax on their profits; they pay corporation tax, though their directors pay income tax under PAYE on their salaries which are, of course, deducted from the company profits for corporation tax purposes. But whatever the structure of the business may be the Inland Revenue will require annual accounts. Companies must, but sole traders and partners need not, have their accounts audited by an accountant holding prescribed qualifications. The expenses of running the business — to quote from the statute, those which are 'wholly and exclusively' incurred for the purpose of the trade — are deducted from profits for tax purposes. But entertaining expenses will not be deductible. An allowable deduction is depreciation affecting the fixed assets of the business. Capital expenditure on business assets may also be relevant for reducing taxable profits; the rules regarding this are, however, subject to change, and you should ascertain the up-to-date position.

Expenses of a revenue type are often incurred before actually starting the business. Provided they were not incurred more than three years previously they may be claimed as deductions. Various other reliefs and exemptions are claimable, and it is a good idea to keep an up-to-date summary of these available for reference.

Value Added Tax

Value Added Tax, unlike the other taxes which have been mentioned, is administered by H.M. Customs and Excise. For the purposes of this tax, provision of goods and services is called 'supply'. A supply may be exempt or taxable, but a taxable supply may be taxable at zero rate! A business which makes only exempt supplies is not registrable for VAT, but one which makes taxable supplies may have to be registered even if some or all of its supplies are zero rated. Consultancy is a taxable supply, and it is not zero rated; but a business with a low annual turnover does not have to be registered for, or pay, VAT. There is also a quarterly turnover limit above which the business must normally register. A business which *is* registered charges VAT on standard rated supplies, which would include consultancy fees.

VAT returns are normally made quarterly. It is a complicated tax, with provisions relating to bad debts, international services and other matters. From the outset, you should find out exactly what your position is regarding VAT and keep proper records.

Anticipation is the key

At the start of your business career it is important to realise that tax is not something over which you have no control, something as inevitable as night and day or summer and winter. But anticipation is necessary if you are to plan well. And significant amounts can be saved without any need to break the law or resort to fraud. Quite simply, tax legislation ordains that in certain circumstances tax will be levied but that there will be various exemptions and reliefs. It is therefore open to you to arrange that the circumstances in which tax is payable do not apply to you and/or to ensure that the exemptions and reliefs *do* apply to you. Planning your affairs in this way is known as 'tax avoidance', whereas escaping tax by breaking the law is 'tax evasion'. No moral or legal issues arise if you do no more than avoid; evasion causes all kinds of problems.

The complexity of the laws, coupled with frequent changes, make tax planning a specialist's job. Most firms of practising accountants have experts who will undertake work of this type for clients, and usually the fees are well justified by the amounts which they can save. But two aspects of accountants' activities need to be watched, although they should not deter you from tax planning. These are:

1. Some accountants lack the moral fibre to deal adequately with contentious issues. They feel that if they press a client's case too hard the taxman may be ill disposed towards them (the accountants) in future. Thus one client's interests are sacrificed so that another's may not be. Accountants who behave in this way do their profession no credit and if this happens the client should ask his solicitor (trained to cope with contentious work) to take over the negotiations.
2. A mindless tax-saver will save tax at all costs. Thus in a family company it may be possible to save tax by voting remuneration to a lightly-taxed member of the family. But will the continuation of that practice eventually result in that person having a loan account so large that he or she will be able to dictate the company's policy by threatening to demand payment?

INSURANCE: THE NECESSARY SAFEGUARD

Many business people give little thought to insurance. Yet quite apart from life assurance on the lives of principals and key employees there are many different types of cover available to them. The ones listed below are particularly relevant to a consultancy practice.

Material damage

The obvious risks are fire and theft, but numerous others — explosion, for instance — are covered under some policies. Many companies offer 'all risks' policies and charge premiums accordingly.

Consequential loss

It is possible to insure against interruption of business. For this purpose it is necessary to estimate the 'gross profit' (as defined under the policy) for the period of insurance. It may be possible to adjust the premium if the actual gross profit (as defined) falls short of the estimate.

Employer's liability

The law requires employers to insure against death of, or bodily injury to, employees. If non-employees — self-employed people perhaps — are likely to be working in the consultancy the possibility of covering them should also be considered.

Public liability

This should cover not only the persons, but also the property, of members of the public who might have cause to make injury or damage claims against the consultancy.

Professional indemnity

The purpose of this is to cover the consultancy against liability for giving wrong or bad advice to clients. It is not always easy to arrange.

Motor vehicles

The law requires a motor policy to cover death of, or injury to, third parties. Insurers usually include cover for such parties' property also, and wider cover— up to 'fully comprehensive' covering accidental damage to the insured person's vehicle — is normally available. It is important to ensure that all vehicles used by the consultancy are insured for business use by all the people who are likely to use them.

It is highly desirable for your consultancy to have a settled policy about insurance. At one extreme, some business people aim at insuring everything they can, and the cost is considerable. At the other, some businesses carry risks which it would be prudent to insure. This is not a matter which should be shrugged off lightly after a discussion with your company's agent. The best person to guide the new consultant through the insurance maze is a reliable broker. And probably the best idea is to insure those risks which, if they were to develop into claims, would result in a crippling loss. Minor risks which the business can easily carry need not be insured. But whatever insurances are arranged the policies should be studied and if anything seems to be amiss it should be taken up with the broker or insurer.

One final observation about insurance: be open and honest with insurers. Suppression of facts or untrue statements can invalidate an insurance policy and entitle an insurer to back out. And sometimes this happens after a claim has actually arisen.

PROFESSIONAL ADVICE

Reference has been made in various parts of this book to the need to take advice. However well versed a consultant you may be in your own discipline there will always be areas in which your knowledge falls far below professional standards. And if you are wise you will choose your advisers with care. Most people in business need an accountant, a solicitor, an insurance adviser and, if property is involved, a surveyor.

Accountants

The main bodies of accountants in England and Wales are the Institute of Chartered Accountants and the Chartered Association of Certified Accountants. There are also organisations of chartered accountants in Scotland and Ireland. Members of these bodies have obtained their qualifications by training and examination; so, as regards cost and management accounting, have the members of the Chartered Institute of Management Accountants. All these accountants are bound by professional codes of discipline and are required to maintain high standards of integrity. That is not to say that non-members of these organisations cannot prepare good accounts or handle tax work; in many cases they are just as scrupulous in their dealings as the members of the recognised bodies. The difference, of course, is that the client cannot in the last resort refer the matter to the accountant's professional body if he does not belong to one.

The main consideration when choosing your accountant is to find one who is well skilled in fulfilling your specific needs. Accounts and tax are usually the needs of the small business; but these are historical functions, and a good accountant should, as we have seen, be able to help his clients with advice for the future and with finance and planning. The skills of the cost and management acountant can be of great value where planning and decision-making are concerned, but relatively few of them practice on their own account.

Solicitors

Here the problems are different. Whereas most accountants are familiar with commercial matters many solicitors are not, and selection of one who is a good business lawyer is therefore very important. A solicitor who spends his day in court defending drug pushers is hardly likely to have the right expertise and will often be unavailable when his advice is urgently required.

Most large legal firms have someone, usually a partner, who can handle commercial work, but there are also some very good people to be found in smaller firms, and it is worth making enquiries among business acquaintances. In a very small town or a village it may be necessary to go to a larger town to find a suitable adviser. This is because there is not enough demand for commercial lawyers in small places to justify their practising there.

Insurance brokers

The world of insurance, which can seem so friendly and straightforward when you insure your life or house through a local agent, becomes a veritable minefield when more complicated cover is wanted or when efforts are being made to establish a claim which insurers are disposed to reject. Guidance is necessary, and a good broker can provide this. It is perhaps unfortunate that brokers, though answerable to their clients, earn their living by commission from insurers. However, that is the way the system has developed, and until it is changed one has to live with it. It is clearly a system which would encourage an unscrupulous broker to ignore the best interests of his client and recommend the insurers who would pay him most in commission. So — don't use an unscrupulous broker!

If he is asked to get the cheapest cover available the broker cannot be blamed if he does exactly that. But the cheapest cover may not be the best buy. If the low premium reflects sound and economical management, well and good, but if it is based on a practice of trying to wriggle out of claims by all manner of legalistic quibbles, then the unhappy insured will not get peace of mind for his premium and indeed may not get anything at all if the quibbles succeed.

At the other extreme, the writer recalls an instance in which a six-figure claim was made late because the insured company had misunderstood the vague wording of the policy and had only realised that a claim could have been made when the time allowed by the policy for making one had expired. Without any legal obligation to pay a penny the insurers settled the claim in full and made no attempt to plead the unsatisfactory wording or the lateness of the claim. The company's brokers had chosen the insurers well — but then the company had chosen its brokers well! Good ones are worth seeking out; they will be independent, knowledgeable, influential and efficient.

Surveyors

The Royal Institution of Chartered Surveyors has within its ranks a large number of talented individuals. Some can draw maps; some can sell houses; and some can tell when the cathedral tower is starting to acquire characteristics usually associated with that at Pisa. Other surveying bodies can boast a great range of talent also. So how is a layman supposed to choose?

As with solicitors there are large firms with specialist departments and smaller ones with specialisations of their own. But in a case in which local knowledge is important it may be wise not to go too far afield. When in doubt the best course is to ask the Institution or one of the other bodies whether it has any members with suitable knowledge practising in the area concerned. But one needs to be specific about the requirements; if a survey is to be made of land in a low-lying area this fact should be stated, so that a surveyor can be found who can advise about possible flooding.

Professional advice: a few pitfalls

Professional advice should always be the best obtainable within the limits of the situation. It is a false economy — a waste of money — to consult someone who does not really understand what he is doing, and the expression 'the blind leading the blind' should be kept in mind. A further point is that professional bodies are not always an unmixed blessing. While there can be little doubt that in many instances they have raised and maintained standards in their respective professions, it is also true that some of their rules have been framed to safeguard their members rather than the public. In case of conflict the professional will obey the rules of his profession which, so far as he is concerned, override his duty to his client. In an extreme case it may be necessary to consult a non-member of a professional body whose only duty is to his client.

Whatever kind of adviser you are using, he should always be given the correct facts. An adviser who has been misled — perhaps deliberately, so that he will give the opinion for which the client hopes — will still charge a fee for his trouble even though his advice, based on the wrong information, may be useless.

A final observation: if an adviser asks his client to sign a form or a document the client should check it first. If something seems to be wrong he should point it out and ask for an explanation.

BOOKS FOR FURTHER REFERENCE

Advertising and PR, Alison Corke, Pan Books (1986)

Contract in a Nutshell, Robert Duxbury, Sweet & Maxwell (1987)

Cost Accounting, W.M. Harper, M & E Handbooks (1987)

Finance for the Non-accountant, L.E. Rockley, Business Books (1984)

Getting to YES, Roger Fisher and William Ury, Hutchinson (1981)

Handbook of Management AZ, Thomas Kempner (ed.), Penguin (1980)

How to Sell a Service, Malcolm McDonald, Heinemann (1986)

Introduction to Company Law, Northey and Leigh, Butterworth (1987)

Management Accounting, W.M. Harper, M & E Handbooks (1982)

Management Made Simple, Coventry and Barker, Heinemann (1981)

Mastering Computers, G.G.L. Wright, Macmillan (1984)

Modern Insurance Law, John Birds, Sweet & Maxwell (1988)

Selwyn's Law of Employment, Norman Selwyn, Butterworth (1985)

Selwyn's Law of Health and Safety at Work, Norman Selwyn, Butterworth (1982)

Tolley's Tax Guide, A. Homer and Rita Burrows, Tolley (annual)

Understanding Company Accounts, Peter Bird, Pitman (1983)

Understanding Property Law, W.T. Murphy and Simon Roberts, Fontana (1987)

Whitaker's Almanack, Whitaker (annual)

Working at Home for Profit, Joanna Johnson, Basil Blackwell (1981)

Working for Yourself, Godfrey Golzen, Kogan Page (1982)

NOTES

NOTES